THE FENCER'S COMPANION

By

CAV. LÉON BERTRAND

DIPLOMÉ L'ACCADEMIA NAZIONALE DI SCHERMA,
NAPOLI (NAPLES);
AUTHOR OF "CUT AND THRUST"

The Naval & Military Press Ltd

2nd Edition

Published by

The Naval & Military Press Ltd

Unit 5 Riverside, Brambleside
Bellbrook Industrial Estate
Uckfield, East Sussex
TN22 1QQ England

Tel: +44 (0)1825 749494

www.naval-military-press.com
www.nmarchive.com

AUTHOR'S PREFACE

In presenting the " Fencer's Companion," I do so in
the hope that it will be accepted as an authoritative
guide by the neophyte who would embrace a noble and
enduring art, the serious student, the practised fencer,
and finally the teacher, for to such is this little volume
dedicated.

Present civilization has long dispensed with swords-
manship in its practical, militant and sometimes sinister
form. Nevertheless, it survives with its traditions and
chivalry intact as the most lasting and beneficial physical
and mental recreation or pursuit. At the inevitable
stage in the practice of secondary games when the
sinews are crying Halt ! the fencer is but proceeding
to the realization of his ambitions, to the full development of his faculties.

Nothing can upset the adage " Practice makes perfect." That being so, I would not wish this little work
to be interpreted as an attempt to usurp the practical
function of the teacher, for it is only with his skilful
co-operation that the ambitious swordsman can climb,
to quote a Service motto, " per ardua ad astra."
A sound theoretical knowledge, however, makes for
proficiency, artistic appreciation and understanding and
enables the student to go forward to meet his instructor
in the cementing of an harmonious association. To this
end I have produced this severely practical manual.
I have compressed much into a little space and it should
come within the reach of all.

I am greatly indebted to S. T. C. Weeks whose arrest-
ing cover design must surely claim attention and to
Lunt Roberts whose clarity of line renders my descrip-
tions almost superfluous. Should our combined efforts
be the means of attracting numbers to the Cause, my
mission will not have been in vain and if my reader
after studying these pages can justly and confidently,
metaphorically speaking, echo the challenge of Rostand's
hero—" at the envoi's end I touch "—I shall be content.

Léon Bertrand

FOREWORD

By Gr. Uff. Nedo Nadi.

Leone Bertrand, che io molto apprezzo come schermidore e come maestro, dopo il suo " Cut and Thrust," pubblica questo " Fencer's Companion." I due libri sono diversi : il primo può esser letto quasi come un piacevole romanzo che sfiora la tecnica senza assumere un tono professorale ; il secondo, invece, è dedicato più specialmente agli schermidori o, in senso più largo, a tutti coloro che all'arte della scherma si appassionano.

Di questo volumetto mi piace la forma e ne approvo la sostanza. Quando Bertrand dice : " To be accepted as a fencer, and consequently an artist, the student must regard technique as his supreme requirement." Bertrand espone con parole sue un mio esatto pensiero. Le molte definizioni che Bertrand offre ai suoi lettori sono d'altronde fra le più precise che mai io abbia letto, come le sue idee sulla guardia, sul ritorno in guardia, sugli esercizi, sul controtempo, sulla tattica dell'assalto e in genere sulle basi fondamentali della scherma, mi sembrano quanto di più accurato e di più moderno si possa leggere oggi in un libro. Tutto è esposto con chiarezza, da un uomo ch'è sicuro di sé. Trattando le tre armi e dando, come si conviene, la parte principale al fioretto, Bertrand intende esser di guida a tutti, al profano come al dilettante, allo schermidore provetto come al maestro. La lettura non sarà inutile per nessuno. Né per l'insegnante che troverà in queste pagine la falsariga d'un metodo perfetto, né per il profano che inevitabilmente sentirà l'attrazione d'un arte nobile e antica, vasta come un mondo.

Nedo Nadi

2, Piazza Santiago del Cile
    (Viale Parioli), Roma.
23 maggio '35/XIII.

iv

" Léon Bertrand, whom I much appreciate as fencer and master, after his ' Cut and Thrust,' publishes this ' Fencer's Companion.' The two books are diverse : the first may be read as a pleasing tale which tones down the technical part without assuming a professorial tone ; the second, instead, is dedicated more specially to fencers, or in a greater sense to all who are devoted to the art of fencing.

" I am pleased with the form and I approve of the substance of this little volume. When Bertrand says, ' To be accepted as a fencer, and consequently an artist, the student must regard technique as his supreme requirement.' Bertrand is expounding with his words my exact thought. The many definitions that Bertrand offers to his readers are besides, among the most precise that I have ever read, as his ideas on the Guard, on the return to Guard, on the exercises, on Counter-time, on the tactics of the bout, and in general on the basic fundamentals of fencing, seem to me to be the most accurate and most modern one can read in a book to-day. All is expounded with clearness, by a man who is sure of himself. Treating of the three weapons and giving, as is proper, the principal part to the foil, Bertrand means to be the guide to everybody, to the uninitiated as well as the amateur, to the experienced fencer and the master alike. The reading will be useless for no one. Neither for the teacher who will find in these pages the guiding line to a perfect method, nor for the uninitiated who will inevitably feel the attraction of an art, noble and ancient, vast as a world."

NEDO NADI.

CONTENTS

PART I

SECTION I

PART ONE

SECTION ONE.

BASES OF INSTRUCTION.
(Foil—Épée—Sabre.)

CHAPTER I.
FUNDAMENTAL PRINCIPLES.

General Considerations.

The Fencer.

The qualities required of the complete swordsman are, on the physical side, technique, speed and stamina ; mentally, he must possess judgment, opportuneness ; and morally, perseverance.

1. **Technique** and precision spell style and mechanical accuracy of movement and, aided by speed, produce perfect co-ordination and facile execution of the various fencing actions.

Technique is the **Master's** first consideration, and in its development lies his foremost duty to his pupil. To be accepted as a **fencer**, and consequently an **Artist**, the student must regard **technique** as his supreme requirement.

I

Stamina is the outcome of a regular and methodical training.

2. **Judgment** is the faculty of adaptation, the judicious choice of tactics and strategy necessary to meet the opposing game.

Opportuneness, *apropos*, means choice of time, the acceptance of the golden and psychological moment to act, to deliver a coup.

3. **Perseverance** is an essential quality of the fencer. With it must be associated patience, enthusiasm and courage. As in all forms of combat, it is not sufficient to know how to conquer ; one must have pre-eminently the will to win.

The fencer will derive an additional benefit physically and add considerably to his versatility if he practises his art with both right and left hands. In this case, his path to ambidexterity will be made easier if he commences with the weaker arm, thus avoiding the sense of an adverse physical balance.

The Armoury : Foil, Épée, Sabre.

4. Each weapon is composed of two principal parts, the blade and the mounting.

The blade, in steel, is divided into two parts, the forte (nearest the guard) and the foible.

The mounting comprises the grip by which the weapon is held, the guard protecting the hand, and the pommel, which is a key to the assembling of the component parts, and acts as a counterweight to the blade.

5. The **Foil** blade is quadrilateral, tapering to a point, which is flattened and can be covered by waxed string or plaster.

The guard may be oval, round, rectangular or " figure eight."

6. The **Épée** blade is fluted and triangular, the point (flattened) being covered, or having a *pointe d'arrêt* affixed thereto.

A cup guard completely shelters the sword-hand.

7. The **Sabre** blade is usually H-sectioned. It has a cutting edge and a base, called the back, while the sides are fluted. It can be straight or slightly curved. Thinning towards the point, the blade becomes double-edged approximately eight inches from the tip. It is a cutting and thrusting weapon.

The guard is in the form of an arc. A cowl which joins one end of the arc to the handle gives complete protection to the hand.

ARTICLE I.

The Grip.

8. The foil and the épée should both be gripped by the thumb and first finger, both practically touching the guard. The thumb should lie along the top of the handle (curving away from the hand), the underside being supported between the first two phalanges of the index.

These are the main manipulative agents. Now apply the remaining digits to the handle. They are thus ready to aid the manipulators in the passing and direction of the point (Fig. 1).

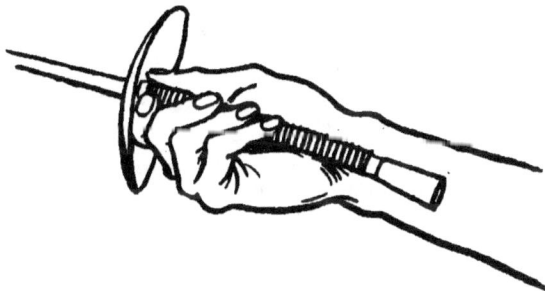

FIG. 1.

There is little difference between the **method of** gripping the foil and épée and that of the sabre. In the latter case, the fingers bring the handle into **final** contact with the heel or ball of the hand. The thumb,

3

first and little fingers are the main controlling members (Fig. 2).

FIG. 2.

In practical demonstration of the grip, the master will naturally at the outset hold the weapon with the bare hand.

ARTICLE II.

The Position of the Guard.

9. The **Guard** is the unique position enabling the fencer to defend and attack with equal facility.

It is therefore the key or fundamental fencing position. On its correctness depends primarily the swordsman's balance and, consequently, the accurate execution of all his movements.

10. To assume the " On Guard " position :—

(1) Place the feet at right angles, the heels touching, the left foot perpendicular to the line of the fencers ; the legs stretched without stiffness, the body erect, shoulders level and relaxed ; the right arm and weapon describing a straight line from shoulder to point in the direction of the right foot, the point about six inches from the floor, the right hand with the nails turned

4

uppermost ; the left arm held naturally, free from the
side with the hand open ; the head erect and facing
the opponent (Fig. 3).

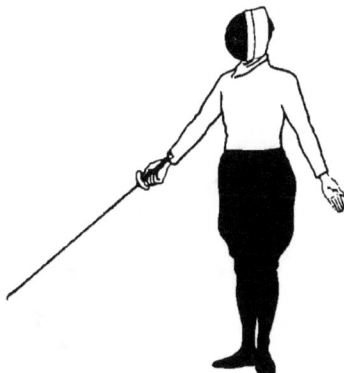

FIG. 3.

(2) Raise the right arm to a level with the eyes,
maintaining the straight line from shoulder to point
(Fig. 4).

FIG. 4.

(3) Bend the right arm, the elbow free from the body, the forearm almost horizontal, the point of the weapon at shoulder level. Simultaneously raise the left arm (elbow at shoulder level), the wrist and hand bent, the whole forming an arc (Fig. 5).

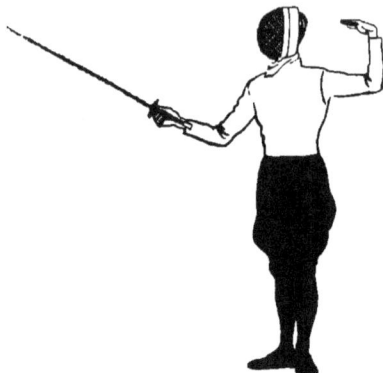

FIG. 5.

(4) Bend the legs (maintaining the trunk erect) so that both knees are directly above the feet (Fig. 6).

FIG. 6.

(5) Advance the right foot and place it flat, opposite the left heel at a distance suitable to the height (two lengths of the fencer's foot separating the heels is a reliable estimate), the right knee vertical with the middle of the foot (Fig. 7).

FIG. 7.

11. **Forming " On Guard " to the Rear.**—Employed especially in épée and sabre fencing, the movements are the same, except in the case of (5), when the left foot is displaced and carried to the appropriate distance behind the right foot, thus enabling the principals to assume " On Guard " out of hitting distance.

12. **General Observation.**—All these directions apply similarly throughout to the left-hander by reading " left " for " right."

Article III.

The Development.

13. The straightening of the arm identifies the attacker. The lunge is the method of delivering the attack ; the whole is the development.

From the " On Guard " position extend the right arm smoothly and quickly, keeping the body absolutely still, the hand in slight supination on a level with the shoulder. Now carry the right foot forward, the heel shaving the ground, and straighten smartly the left leg. At the same time drop the left arm to a position more or less parallel with the left leg, the hand open with fingers straight and together, the thumb uppermost. The right foot remains flat, the knee vertical with the middle of the foot, the body lightly forward, the hand very slightly above the level of the shoulder.

FIG. 7A.

14. **Observations.**—It is essential that :—

    (a) The lunge be preceded always by the straightening of the arm. This is a cardinal rule in the execution of the attack "Point first" is a maxim never to be forgotten. With the attack at its swiftest, the hand should have a fractional precedence of the foot. This is the correct co-ordination.

    (b) The straightening of the right arm should be a natural and unobtrusive action, independent of the shoulder.

    (c) In the lunge, the right heel alights on the floor first.

    (d) The left foot remains flat as it is the left leg that imparts the thrust.

ARTICLE IV.

The Return to Guard.

15. To return to guard : Thrust back with the right heel and, bending the left leg, carry the weight of the body on to the left leg before replacing the right foot in its original position, when the weight is again equally distributed. Simultaneously raise the left arm to its former position and progressively bend the right arm, the point in line at the outset to cover the return to guard.

16. The return to guard can, in certain exceptional cases, be effected by bringing up the left foot (while on the lunge) to the required distance behind the right, the latter remaining in its place.

ARTICLE V.

To Gain, To Break Ground (Advance, Retreat)

17. **Ground** is the maximum distance in which a fencer, by lunging, can reach his opponent.

To **make** or **break ground** means, therefore, manœuvring oneself within or out of the reach of the opponent, the distance being calculated in relation to the fencer himself in the first case, and to the adversary in the second.

18. **To Gain Ground.**—From the position of "On Guard" advance the right foot, the body erect, followed by the left to its distance, both feet grazing the floor, the legs remaining bent throughout.

19. **To Break Ground.**—Move the left foot back, followed by the right to its distance.

Observation.

(a) It is important to maintain the length of the stance both in advancing and retreating. The **Advance** is a stealthy, smooth movement, and only a very short pace forward should be necessary.

(b) The **Retreat** is a freer and more definite movement. Complete immobility of the trunk must be maintained in both operations.

ARTICLE VI.

Appel—Rassemblement—Salute.

20. The **Appel** is the action of sharply striking the floor with the right foot. It may have the effect of startling or momentarily disturbing the opponent, lending colour to an attack which is in reality a false one.

21. **Rassemblement.**—This is the movement immediately preceding the final salute (see Fig. 4), and is made by bringing the right foot to the left (and *vice versa*), coming to an upright position.

22. The Salute.—The salute is performed in three movements—(*a*) As in Fig. 4 ; (*b*) bend the right arm, the forearm and blade vertical, the guard on a level with the chin, the fingers facing the body (Fig. 8) ; (*c*) lower the weapon to the position of Fig. 3.

FIG. 8.

CHAPTER II.

LINES.

---

23. **Lines** are space-judged in relation to the fencer's hand, in which the latter manœuvres his weapon.

There are four lines—the high line ; the low line ; the right line, called the outside line ; and the left line, known as the inside line.

ARTICLE I.

Fencing Positions.

24. The hand can assume a certain number of positions between two given limits. These limits are (*a*) with the fingers uppermost ; (*b*) with the knuckles uppermost. In the former case the hand is in **supination**, in the latter **pronation.**

In relation to the hand there are three positions of the blade—(1) The point above the hand ; (2) The point on a level with the hand ; (3) The point below the hand.

Combinations in themselves of these various positions of the hand constitute **fencing positions**, which serve as the basis for parries.

These positions are eight in number. They are called **Prime, Seconde, Tierce, Quarte, Quinte, Sixte, Septime** and **Octave,** and are described and illustrated as follows :—

25. **Prime** (pronation).—Protecting high and inside

lines ; the forearm horizontal, the point lower than the hand (Figs. 9 and 10).

FIG 9.   FIG. 10.

26. **Seconde** (pronation).—The hand to the right, point lower than the hand, protecting outside and low lines (Figs. 11 and 12).

FIG. 11.   FIG. 12.

27. Tierce (pronation).—Hand to the right, **point** higher than the hand, protecting high and **outside** lines (Figs. 13 and 14).

FIG. 13   FIG 14.

28. Quarte (supination).—Hand to the left, lightly turned, point higher than the hand, protecting high and inside lines (Figs. 15 and 16).

FIG. 15.   FIG. 16.

29. **Quinte** (pronation).—Hand to the left, point slightly higher than the hand, protecting the inside and low lines (Figs. 17 and 18).

FIG. 17.　　　　　　　　FIG. 18.

30. **Sixte** (supination).—Hand to the right, point higher than the hand, protecting outside and high lines (Figs. 19 and 20).

FIG. 19.　　　　　　　　FIG. 20

31. **Septime** (supination).—Hand to the left, point lower than the hand, protecting the low and inside lines (Figs. 21 and 22).

FIG. 21.   FIG. 22.

32. **Octave** (supination).—Hand to the right, point lower than the hand, protecting low and outside lines (Figs. 23 and 24).

FIG. 23.   FIG. 24.

NOTE.—It will be seen that in the case of pronation, with the exception of **Quinte**, the pommel is on the outside of the wrist.

Further, to simplify the arrangement of these positions, they may be regarded as four in number, each possessing **pronate** and **supinate** editions both of which serve a similar defensive purpose. Thus, **Prime** and **Quarte** are complementary, **Seconde** and **Octave**, **Tierce** and **Sixte**, and finally, **Quinte** and **Septime**.

ARTICLE II.

Engagement.

33. The **Engagement** is the action of joining by crossing the opposing blade. There are as many engagements as positions—*i.e.*, engagement of Quarte, Sixte, Tierce, etc.

The **Engagement** is primarily a preliminary precaution in that it at once renders the direct thrust abortive. It permits of a close acquaintance with the adversary, of an idea of his disposition and his fingering, and adds security to all attacks on his blade.

34. The **Change of Engagement** is an engagement made in the opposite line to the one previously taken. In the high line this change is made by passing the point under the opposing blade. In the low line the point is passed over the opposing blade. The **Double Engagement** is the action of two changes made in quick succession.

In defence the change of engagement renders the blade elusive to the adversary, and therefore hinders his offensive.

In attack it is (the double engagement in particular) a measure of precaution with the object—on the advance, for instance—of immobilising the opponent, of fixing his attention to the blade as a cover while gaining ground.

The change of engagement can also be used to provoke an adverse action —*i.e.*, to draw an attack.

Absence of Blade.

35. The absence of blade has two objects. In defence : To avoid force or pressure on the blade, and thus generally to counterbalance any physical inferiority of the hand. In attack : To provoke an adverse action. In this case the action is called the **Invite.**

SECTION TWO.

Foil Fencing.

CHAPTER I.

OFFENSIVE ACTIONS.

The Particular Convention of the Foil.

36. The Foil is an instrument of study conceived to facilitate the teaching of fencing with the point, such teaching to develop to the highest degree the passing and progress of that point.

The shortest route or path to the objective that can be described by the point is a straight line directed by the sword-arm at shoulder level. It suffices, therefore, to reduce all conventions which may have existed in the past to one alone, that of restricting the surface to be attained to an area offering the maximum scope and concentration around the shortest line of objective.

An ideal target is one in which this surface is limited to the trunk bounded by the hips and the collar-bone.

Amateur fencing legislators have seen fit, however, to extend the target to the bounds delineated in Fig. 25.

FIG. 25.

Thus, all hits scored within the limits illustrated above are valid, and any point arriving outside these bounds suffices to terminate the phase and to annul any consecutive riposte or counter-riposte.

ARTICLE I.

Simple Attack.

37. The attack is an offensive action comprising the development. It is simple or compound. There are three simple attacks :—The **Direct Thrust**, the **Disengagement,** and the **Cut-over.**

38 The **Direct Thrust** is delivered in the line of engagement left open by the opponent. (To apply the direct thrust. See pages 7 and 8.)

39. The **Disengagement** is delivered from the line of engagement to another line by the shortest possible route.

To disengage : Pass the point under the adversary's blade into the required line with a **progressive** movement of the arm, then lunge, taking care that the point has a fractional precedence of the right foot.

A disengagement from the low line would be made by passing the point over the opposing blade.

40. The **Cut-over** is a disengagement made from the high line into the opposite high line by passing the point over the opposing blade.

To cut over : With thumb and index finger (slightly relaxing the remaining digits and slightly bending the wrist) raise the blade, always retaining contact with the adversary's blade, until the opposing point is reached. Regain full grip and drop the point into the other line with a progressive movement of the arm, lunge.

Compound Attack.

41. When an attack is preceded by one or more **Feints of Attack,** it is called a compound attack.

A **Feint of Attack** is made with the object of drawing the opposing blade into one line in order to score in another. It must have such an appearance of reality that, taken for the attack itself, it provokes a parry.

It is succeeded at the appropriate moment by a movement which deceives this parry.

The speed of this deception is naturally dependent upon that of the parry.

42. An attack composed of a **Feint of Disengagement deceiving a simple or direct parry** is termed " **One-Two.**" If it be composed of two feints of disengagement it becomes " **One-Two-Three.**"

When the attack consists of a feint of disengagement deceiving a **circular** parry, it is identified briefly as a " **Double.**"

43. To **deceive** is the term generally applied to the movement whereby the blade eludes a defensive action. One speaks particularly of a **Counter Disengagement** when this action takes the form of a **counter** parry.

Escaping contact with the opposing blade when the opponent is making an offensive motion is known in French as *derober*. The reader or student will have to remain content with this term, as there is no adequate equivalent in English.

Preparations of Attack.

44. The attack may be facilitated and, to a certain extent secured, by various preliminary movements called **Preparations of Attack.**

The **several** objects of these movements are to divert the opposing point with more or less force by means of the **Beat,** or pressure, which uncovers the opponent for the direct thrust or feint thereof, or draws a response to be deceived, to dispose of the adverse blade with violence by means of the *froissement,* which may be identified as a " forceful graze," and finally, to ward off the blade and at the same time to dominate it by means of **Opposition,** the **Bind** and **Envelopment.**

These **Preparations of Attack** may be divided under two headings—(a) Attacks on the blade ; (b) Taking the blade. The *coulé* (see para. No. 52) and the false attack may come within the scope of this article.

Attacks on the Blade.

45. There are three attacks on the blade—the **Beat** the **Pressure,** and the **Froissement.**

46. The **Beat** and the **Pressure** should be executed —primarily by compression of the thumb and index finger—crisply and decisively when followed im mediately by the direct thrust ; with lightness when employed to provoke a response. They are made on the foible of the opposing blade.

47. The **Froissement** is a prolonged pressure from foible to forte in which the opposing blade is brushed brusquely aside, the executant's point finishing approximately at its original elevation. It is more effective when delivered on an extended arm.

Taking the Blade.

48. Taking the blade is an action upon the opposing steel with the object of warding off the point and at the same time dominating the adversary's blade. It is, of course, made with the forte against the **foible** and for preference on a straight arm.

Care must be taken (a) to administer controlled resistance to the blade lest the point be carried away out of line ; (b) to ensure that the movement is complete before delivering the attack.

When the action is sustained to the end of the attack itself, it is called an **Attack of Authority**.

A compound attack may follow the taking of the blade. In this case it may be categorized as an "accentuated attack on the blade."

The blade may be taken in three ways :—(a) By **Opposition** ; (b) By **Binding** ; (c) By **Enveloping**.

49. Taking the blade by **Opposition** is a progressive opposition in the line of, or following an engagement, and is continued until the attack.

50. Taking the blade by **Binding** is to gather the blade and bring it from the high line to the low, and *vice versa*.

When this action is employed as a riposte, it is known as the **Croisé**, in that it crosses from one line to another, *e.g.* from **Quarte** to **Octave** ; **Sixte** to **Septime**.

51. The **Envelopment** brings back the adversary's blade to the line in which it was previously situated, both points describing a complete circle.

52. The **Coulé** (graze) is the action of gliding or grazing the blade along the adversary's until the arm is straightened in preparation of, or to lodge, an attack.

53. The **False Attack** may be simple or compound, more or less pronounced, in any case never completely delivered. It is a tentative attack made with the object of animating the opponent, stirring him into activity to discover his intentions, reactions, the parries he favours, in order to counter the former and deceive the latter as the case may be.

The movement should have all the appearance of a genuine attack if it is to draw from the opponent a parry or a parry and riposte, to be countered by a counter-riposte (para. No. 66), a remise (para, No. 60), or a reprise (para. No. 59), according to the case.

On the other hand, the **False Attack** must be less pronounced against an adversary who, one senses, is not relying on the parry for his defence, since it must provoke at the outset a time-thrust (para. No. 55) or a tension (para. No. 57), with the object of operating in counter-time against him. These tactics should prove more effective if accompanied by the **Appel** (para. No. 20), or the **Advance** (para. No. 18).

Counter-attacks.

54. The **Counter-attack** is, generally speaking, an attacking movement which may or may not comprise the lunge, and is executed on the opposing offensive. There are three forms of **Counter-attack**, the **Time-thrust**, the **Stop-thrust** and the **Tension**.

55. The **Time-thrust**, it will readily be appreciated, is a stroke best delivered on a compound attack against which the former gains one or more units of time (*e.g.*, the direct thrust executed on an opposing "One-Two-Three.")

56. When the counter-attack is launched on the advance of the opponent it checks an offensive at its inception. Hence it is called a **Stop-thrust.**

57. If the opportunity be seized at the right moment, the counter-attack may be delivered on a simple offensive. This is accomplished merely by straightening the arm. Thus, this movement may forestall a disengagement or cut-over from quarte to the line of sixte, etc., and it will be seen that this single action discharges at one stroke the dual obligation of parry and riposte. As its nature implies, this form of counter-attack is known as the **Tension.**

58. The **Redouble** consists of delivering a second attack immediately after the first in the same line or in another. It is a renewal of the offensive against an adversary who has parried but fails to riposte, or against one who has avoided being hit by retreating. In the former case the renewal is preceded by a retaking (reprise) of the guard to the rear (see para. No. 15) and by a reprise to the fore (see para. No. 16) in the latter.

59. The **Reprise** (of the attack) is an offensive movement executed without rising from the lunge after an opposing parry not succeeded by a riposte.

General Observation.—The circumstances in which the **Redouble** and **Reprise** are executed are very similar, especially where the **Reprise and Redouble** (reprise of the guard to the rear) are concerned. It may be that the **Redouble** offers more freedom of action for a second attack of increased vigour and speed, but the **Reprise** is to be particularly recommended for its economy of motion and element of surprise.

Consider the following illustration. The attacker launches an attack avowedly false ; the defender hesitates to riposte, suspecting that his reply is being drawn to provide a counter-riposte. This moment of irresolution on the part of the defence gives the attacker excellent scope for what may be termed a piece of opportunism. For example : (a) Attacker disengages into Sixte and is parried by Counter-Quarte. In ensuing momentary pause, attacker makes reprise by disengagement into low line (*en main seconde*) ; (b) Disengagement in Quarte line parried by Counter-Sixte, reprise by disengagement. The defender may, on the other hand, decide to make a compound riposte, in which case the momentary pause gives an alert attacker an equal opportunity to profit by a **Remise.** The above examples suggest the kindred nature of the **Reprise** and the **Remise.**

60. The **Remise** is a time-thrust, and is executed on the lunge against a compound or indirect riposte, or after an inadequate parry not followed by a reply. As its name implies, the action consists of replacing the point after its deflection and pressing it home anew. This movement may also be operated from the position of " On Guard," when it would be made following a compound counter-riposte.

Observation.—So far as the compound riposte by disengagement, and with the possible addition of the cut-over, is concerned, the **Remise** is best effected following a Quarte or Counter-Quarte parry, when the Remise provides at the same time a natural opposition which is similarly found in the case of Septime or Counter-Septime succeeded by a disengagement into Octave.

A **Remise** following a disengagement or cut-over from any other line will be found to be an unsafe proposition, not only in point of time, but in view of the opposition herein which becomes more or less of a contortion.

61. **Counter-Time is a most valuable sense, faculty,** or **mood.** It is the strategy by which an opponent is induced or provoked to attack *in tempo*, with the object of counter-timing or alternatively taking possession of the opposing blade or detaching it and executing a subsequent attack or riposte.

With this object in view, a fencer is said to " move in counter time."

CHAPTER II.

DEFENSIVE ACTIONS.

Article I. Parries.

    ,,   II. Ripostes—Counter-Ripostes.

ARTICLE I.

Parries.

62. The **Parry** is the fencer's positive defence. It is the action of turning aside or diverting the attacker's blade.

There are two kinds of parries : The **Direct** or **Simple Parry**, and the **Circular** or **Counter Parry**.

The **Direct** or **Simple Parry** deflects the opposing blade, leaving it outside the same line in which it was delivered.

The **Circular** or **Counter Parry** seeks the blade in the line it is presented to regain contact and deflect it in the opposite line, the point describing a complete circle.

Observation.—The **Simple Parry** is naturally at the outset the easier of execution, but the **Counter**, having regard to the stationary position of the hand, spells greater stability and control. They may be regarded respectively as the **instinctive** and **acquired** parries, and for this reason the **Counter** movement should be at once developed until the initial and early partiality for the **Simple** parry has worn off.

63. Whether direct or circular, the parry may be executed in two different ways—by **Opposition**, by **Detachment**.

(*a*) To parry by **Opposition** is to divert the blade by pressure without losing contact.

(*b*) To parry by **Detachment** is to deflect the blade by a crisp beat.

c   **25**

64. Each parry has its counter. There are eight parries executed from the positions of **Prime, Seconde Tierce,** etc. (see paras. Nos. 25 to 32).

Ripostes—Counter-Ripostes.

65. The **Riposte** is a reply to an unsuccessful attack, and is therefore to be regarded as the sequel to a successful parry. When a fencer safely defends himself from an offensive he has the right of reply.

There are three kinds of **Ripostes—Direct, Compound** and **Delayed.**

The **Direct Riposte** is the stroke delivered immediately after the parry in the same line.

The **Compound Riposte** is an indirect reply such as the riposte by disengagement, cut-over, " One-Two," etc.

It is a **Delayed Riposte** when the stroke deceives an initial counter-parry or awaits an opposing reaction in a line other than direct.

66. When a reply is parried and is followed by an answering riposte, this latter stroke is termed the **Counter-Riposte.**

General Observation.—The necessity for developing a swift riposte cannot be too highly emphasised— it is self-evident. It at once brings relief to the defence. Consider the case of a defender failing to reply. He lays himself open to a renewal of the offensive and may conceivably succumb eventually to the persistence of the attacker.

It is essential that the **Direct Riposte** be assiduously practised. It is above all the antidote to the **Remise.** Following in particular the parry by detachment, it should form a spontaneous, impulsive movement in which the operation is assisted by the action of rebound. Thus the movement should have all the speed of elasticity and be made from complete immobility. So much so that the attacker will have no option but to remain on the lunge and rely on his reflex arm motion to defend himself.

CHAPTER III.

COMBAT.

Article I. Principal Tactics.

,, II. The Bout.

ARTICLE I.

Principal Tactics.

67. **Tactics in fencing mean the judicious employment of the various processes of attack and defence appropriate to the opposing game with the full utilisation of one's physical resources.**

68. The general principles may be summed up thus : **Offensive—only the rational offensive** which looks ahead, counteracts and paralyses the adverse attack, enabling the attacker to retain all the time mental and physical alertness, **guarantees success.**

Do not expend your mental energy needlessly in exploring a labrynth of complication. Do not elaborate nor dissipate your physical strength in launching attacks out of time, nor at such distance that they are pre-destined to failure.

Let simplicity be the keynote of your offensive. Do not despise the direct attack, the attack on the blade, the movement preceded by one feint, the *prise de fer*, etc. **Simple attacks are the best.**

Remember that on the efficacy of your simple attacks depends your strategy, your plan of campaign. They heighten the impression of your subsequent feints and render your adversary responsive to them.

Attack when your opponent is pre-occupied, when he is preparing his offensive, on his advance, his absence of blade, his engagement and change of same.

These are the golden moments in which to act, but the opportunities can only be seized by an unceasing concentration and vigilance.

Develop your judgment of time. **The choice of time is the supreme factor in the success of an offensive.** Even faultless technique and lightning rapidity will fail if the attack be launched **out of time.**

Regard your opponent's concentration in terms of a graph, and attack in the depressions, in his moments of irresolution.

Conserve your energy, but **attack decisively, confidently and with a single mind.** There should be no compromise. A movement that bears the stamp of uncertainty, apprehension at the thought of possible failure, is already doomed, and it is a waste of time and energy.

Do not seek the low line until the high line (the primary region) has been sufficiently assailed so that the maximum effect may be given to the element of surprise.

Use the cut-over sparingly and with the utmost discretion. It is a disconcerting and intimidatory stroke, but as the purist would rightly have it, it is unprogressive.

In all cases, whether the stroke succeeds or not, recover in order. Furthermore, it may frequently be a prudent step when breaking off the exchanges to retire out of distance to regain composure.

69. **Defensive.**—It is difficult to lay down arbitrary principles or to generalise under this clause. **Above all, do not let your defence be a passive, supine one,** permitting your adversary to creep in ; do not give him time to prepare or to lodge attacks at his own leisure. In short, do not let him have his own way.

To render your defence as impenetrable as possible, eschew all unnecessary movements—the superfluous or hasty parry, the unconsidered change of line, etc., and **delay your parry until the last moment.**

You will, of course, vary your parries as much as possible. Combine them judiciously with the time and stop thrusts to check and tone down your opponent's initiative and enterprise.

In your positive defence—that is, your protection by the parry—use more often than not the counter as your first line of defence.

The Bout.

70. If you would fence intelligently you would do well to precede actual hostilities by a rapid mental stocktaking of your adversary in order to initiate a plan of campaign.

Firstly, to avoid being taken by surprise, you will assume the " On Guard " position out of lunging distance. In your first survey you will note his general deportment, his style, and particularly his stance, to give you some idea of his length and reach. You will then observe the position of his hand, the inclination of the trunk, the extent to which the arm is lengthened and the legs bent. These points will indicate in a measure his flexibility and mobility.

From your first exchanges strive to discover as soon as possible whether he relies on his legs or his hand ; on his physique or his technique. Observe his preference or otherwise for the simple or compound attack, whether it is accompanied or not by the advance. Note if his system of defence is varied, is fortified by the use of counter-attacks, if all lines are equally guarded.

When this mental reconnaissance has been made and the fencer has drawn his conclusions, it suffices for him to put them into operation. Having conceived a project, he must act upon it as whole-heartedly as possible, and with all the decision at his command. He should not let his opponent sense that his attacks have a tentative or experimental quality.

Because you find certain strokes peculiarly effective, do not develop a marked partiality for them. They may eventually be your strong suit in match or competition, but **your art is learnt in the salle** where you will seek to enlarge and vary your game by adapting your methods to those of your adversary, and by trading on his defects and weaknesses.

Although each adversary provides a fresh study, there are outstanding types of opponents, distinct by reason of their individuality, physique or technique, against whom it is advisable to employ certain and special tactics.

For instance, **against the very tall man** you will wage a harassing and mobile battle. In attack you will seek, under cover of a constant contact with his blade to advance well within distance where his superior reach becomes an embarrassment. In defence you will be more elusive than positive.

On the other hand, **if you have a decided advantage in height and length,** you will be aloof. You will keep him constantly out of distance. You will not readily join in protracted exchanges, especially if he possesses an excellent hand, and by your longer reach you will subdue his advances and preparations by the time and stop thrusts.

Finally, you will not neglect the direct riposte. These two types emphasize above all **the importance of the judgment of distance.**

If you are faced with **a lethargic, stolid opponent,** whose definition seems vague and uncertain, impress upon him your authority and decision, and in your compound attacks take care that the speed of your preliminary movements corresponds with that of his parries.

You will exploit to the full **a nervous impressionable fencer** and increase his tension by incessant skirmishes, without, however, committing yourself.

There is **the foilist who systematically refuses the engagement of steel.** Bring him to an acquaintance with your blade by false attacks, and, above all, the direct feint.

Lastly, there are two types of fencers against whom you will proceed with a more definite policy. They are the **left-hander and the exponent of the Italian school.**

71. **A bout between left and right-handers** brings Quarte with its, comparatively speaking, physical superiority into play against Sixte. Thus, the left-hander will, more often than not, seek to impose this greater authority behind the parries of Quarte and its counter. It would be unwise, therefore, to submit too frequently to these defences. If one must challenge them, a " One-Two " once or twice deceiving the counter, or a treble disengagement, as the case may be, may prove a judicious move. This advice applies similarly to the left-hander.

Mutual recognition of this change of perspective should ensure the frequent execution after the parries of Sixte and Counter-Sixte, of ripostes by the Disengagement, by the Cut-over and by the Double, involving as a counter-stroke the use of the Remise, the Delayed Riposte, and the Reply in the low line.

72. In advising proceedings **against the exponent of the Italian system**, one must not forget that the present-day Italian foilist is a modified type of his school. In fact, the greater reliance upon footwork, the adoption of modelled handles fitting into the hand and completed by a strap, by the French foilist, the greater attention paid by the Italian to finger-work, and to evasion rather than the domination of the opposing blade, are signs that the two schools are approaching unification.

Yet the Italian system may truthfully be said to be a more militant one. The characteristic Italian fencer, armed with a foil bound to the wrist, affects a less pronounced guard in which there is a greater reduction in the angle of deflection. Consequently his arm, in the initial position, is practically extended, His security of grip and his partiality for pronation (Tierce instead of Sixte, Seconde in place of Octave) give him added decision and power in his parries and attacks on the blade. This apparent advantage is offset in defence by a comparative loss of flexibility and ease of arm movement, which is, however, redeemed to a certain extent by a greater reliance on mobility in footwork.

In the light of these facts your **offensive** must be prudent and reasoned. You will wield rather an elusive blade, thus avoiding falling under the domination of his harsher contact. Particular heed must be paid to your choice of time, lest you impale yourself on his Time or Stop thrusts, these strokes being well favoured by him. The guard of your Italian adversary leaves, at the outset, little scope for attacks in the high line. You will therefore naturally prefer the low, in which the deception of the Mezzo Cercio (Septime) parry calls for your special attention. It is as facile as Quarte to him. Indeed, Counter-Quarte, Septime is perhaps his favourite method of defence.

You will need to maintain a very lively and active **defence** against the Italian attack. More often than not the latter is executed on the advance and on the blade ; in consequence, there should be ample opportunity for the delivery of Time and Stop thrusts and, above all, the *derobement*. **Avoid contact** as much as possible in the preliminary exchanges. Give a constant thought to Time and Counter-Time.

CHAPTER IV.

THE MASTER—METHOD OF TEACHING—SERIES OF EXERCISES

ARTICLE I.

The Master.

73. Briefly, the successful *Maître d'Armes, Maestro di Scherma*, or Fencing-Master, must possess qualities and qualifications which may be summarised thus: **Knowledge, Personality, Psychological Understanding.**

74. **Knowledge.**—From this qualification the master derives his faculty of expounding and teaching his art. Allied to this, there is a distinct technique apart from the actual execution of the countless strokes and movements which comprise the term fencing. This technique of the teacher lies in a general way in the sympathetic accompaniment of the blade in the development of the pupil's attack, and the accurate and precise presentation of the point in the construction of his defence.

75. **Personality.**—By this is meant the degree of authority and the sense of discipline imposed upon the pupil by which the master may extract from him the maximum concentration. To this may be added the **Power of Communication,** almost a mesmeric quality which spurs and stimulates the pupil, drawing from him his best mental and physical endeavour.

76. **Psychological Understanding.**—This sense is knowledge of the pupil, the study of, and adaptation to, his exceptional requirements, the exercise of **tact** and the minimum concession to his idiosyncrasies.

Method of Teaching.

77. Since the object of this work is to provide a manual practical in its simplicity, rather than a dissertation upon the art, you will rely almost entirely on **supination**, although movements finishing *en main seconde* must not be overlooked. Broadly speaking, the accompanying series of exercises are intended as a guide to a *gradatim* study, and need not necessarily be rigidly adhered to in all their details.

There is nothing more exacting than a fencing lesson. You will therefore be discreet in your demands upon your pupil's energy. By all means extract from him his utmost endeavour, but let it be a tax on his resources willingly accepted and progressive with the increase in his stamina.

Alternate the movements of attack and defence as much as possible. Ring the changes constantly to keep him mentally alert. A too insistent repetition of a particular stroke or exercise tends to create monotony, with a resultant decline in his concentration and interest.

Explain carefully and in simple language the "raison d'etre" and the "modus operandi" of each movement.

It is essential that your pupil retains mental composure ; that he makes his departure from complete immobility, and that he properly understands your particular instruction. **You will therefore check anticipation, a hurried and ill-timed commencement, by leaving a sufficient interval between your command and your movement necessary to provoke the required stroke.**

Throughout the lesson impose the maximum correction upon your pupil in his style and movements. Never pass a technical imperfection, nor proceed until the stroke is executed to your complete satisfaction.

Your pupil will naturally make his movements by numbers first, and then without analysis. **Precision before speed always,** but remember that a too frequent analysis must necessarily affect his suppleness.

You will, from the outset, devote the maximum attention to your pupil's finger-work. Ensure throughout that his point movements emanate from the fingers. **Instantly suppress all rigidity of the arm and contraction of the shoulder.**

Develop your pupil's Sixte position and parries so as to check any initial preference for those of Quarte, a partiality usually evinced by the beginner owing to the greater physical ease of the latter.

Change the line after each exercise. Supplement the attack with the change of engagement, double change, etc.

Do not insist upon a too constant repetition of the lunge by reason of its physical demand. This, again, may adversely affect suppleness. Neither must your pupil be kept too long at full stretch in the practice of the counter-riposte.

To prevent the pupil from becoming static and to avoid unnecessary fatigue, keep him constantly on the move with frequent commands of " Advance " and " Retreat." Develop to the utmost your pupil's judgment of distance. Give him ample opportunity for attacks on the advance, the redouble, parries and ripostes in retiring, etc. etc.

To perfect his passing of the point, do not hesitate to proceed as far as attacks of three feints (independent of series V), such as " Double-double," quadruple disengagement, " One-two-three " and deceiving the counter, " Double and one-two," " One-two deceiving the counter and disengaging," " Treble and disengagement."

Without neglecting the Direct Riposte, which should always be practised in a greater ratio, vary your pupil's replies as much as possible. Make him riposte, for instance, by the disengagement, " One-two-three," and Double from Quarte and Counter-Quarte; by " One-two," and Double and disengagement from Sixte and Counter-Sixte ; the disengagement into the low region from the Sixte line, and similarly from Quarte *en main seconde*, etc. etc.

When your pupil is sufficiently advanced it is frequently a good idea **during the course of the lesson to introduce one or two brief periods in which he is permitted to engage you for a maximum of two hits.** It tends to relieve the exactions of the lesson and gives the pupil a sense of responsibility in granting him the liberty of acting on his own initiative, thereby increasing his interest. Give him every facility for developing his offensive by clearly defined indications, at the same time correct any badly executed movement such, for instance, as a bent-arm attack.

Immediately reproduce the particular stroke as part of the lesson. Fully impress upon him that **it is not the hit that counts so much as the manner of its accomplishment.**

You will devise between your pupils' exercises of a progressive and reciprocal nature. They should, however, be of short duration as they lack the authority and discipline of the master.

Finally you will authorize a bout between them. You will select to start with contestants of approximately similar physique and strength. As often as possible the bout will be contested in your presence and under your strict supervision. You will intervene constantly to correct faults and to give the necessary tactical explanations and advice.

ARTICLE III

Series of Exercises.

FIRST SERIES : FUNDAMENTAL POSITIONS.

Preliminary Exercises (with and without Analysis).

Assume the " On Guard " position in five movements.
Advance.
Retreat.
Extend the Arm.
Lunge.
Return to Guard.
Engage the Blade.
Change the Engagement.
Fencing Positions.*
Reassemble.
Salute.

* The fencing positions should be assumed thus :—(1) Supination ; (2) Pronation, and in the following order : Quarte, Sixte, Septime, Octave, Prime Seconde, Tierce and Quinte.

Analysed.   *Without Analysis.*

The Direct Thrust.

*On my absence of blade—   Lunge.
   Extend the arm—Lunge.

The Disengagement.

Feint of disengagement (or   Disengage (or disengage
   pass under/over and ex-   into the low/high line).
   tend)—Lunge.

The Cut-over.

Cut over and extend—   Cut over.
   Lunge.

Parries to Meet the Above Attacks
(with direct Riposte).

(From the Engagement of Quarte.)

Parry of the Direct Thrust.

Analysed.   *Without Analysis.*

*Open the line—On my   Quarte (or Counter-Sixte)
   lunge, parry Quarte (or
   Counter-Sixte)—Riposte.

Parry of the Disengagement.

On my disengagement,   Counter-Quarte (or Sixte)•
   parry Counter-Quarte
   (or Sixte)—Riposte.

Parry of the Cut-over.

On my cut-over, parry   Counter-Quarte (or Sixte).
   Counter - Quarte (or
   Sixte)—Riposte.

* Assuming the engagement of blades the direct thrust
cannot arise, hence the preparatory movement.

THIRD SERIES : ATTACKS COMPOSED OF ONE FEINT.

(Feint of the Direct Thrust, Disengagement, Cut-over.)
Parries to meet these Attacks and Simple and Compound Ripostes.

ATTACKS.		PARRIES AND VARIED RIPOSTES.
Analysed.	*Without Analysis.*	
From the engagement of Quarte :		
I open the line— Feint of the direct thrust, I parry Quarte, deceive, lunge	Feint of the direct thrust, disengage	Quarte, Sixte (or Counter-Quarte).
—Feint of the direct thrust, I parry Quarte, deceive into the low line, lunge	Feint of the direct thrust, disengage low line	Quarte, Septime.
—Feint of the direct thrust, I parry Counter-Sixte, deceive the counter, lunge	Feint of the direct thrust, counter-disengage	Counter · Sixte, Quarte (twice Counter-Sixte).
—Feint of the direct thrust (from Sixte), I parry Counter-Quarte, deceive into the low line lunge	Feint of the direct thrust, counter-disengage low	Counter-Quarte, Septime.
Feint of disengagement, I parry Sixte, deceive, lunge	One-Two	Sixte, Quarte (or Counter-Sixte).
Feint of disengagement, I parry Quarte, deceive into the low line (*en main seconde*), lunge	One-Two into the low line	Quarte, Septime.
Feint of disengagement, I parry Counter-Quarte, deceive, lunge	Double	Counter · Quarte, Sixte (twice Counter-Quarte)

37

ATTACKS.		PARRIES AND VARIED RIPOSTES.
Analysed.	*Without Analysis.*	
Feint of disengagement, I parry Counter-Quarte, deceive into the low line, lunge	Double into the low line	Counter-Quarte, Septime.
Feint of disengagement low, I parry Septime, deceive into the high line, lunge	Feint of disengagement low, disengage high	Septime, Quarte.
Feint of disengagement low, I parry Septime, deceive into the low line, lunge	Feint of disengagement low, disengage low	Septime, Octave (or Counter-Septime).
Feint of the Cut-over, I parry Sixte, deceive, lunge	Cut-over, disengage	Sixte, Quarte (or Counter-Sixte).
Feint of the Cut-over, I parry Quarte, deceive into the low line, lunge	Cut-over low line	Quarte, Septime.
Feint of the Cut-over, I parry Counter-Quarte, deceive, lunge	Cut-over and counter-disengage	Counter - Quarte, Sixte (twice Counter-Quarte).
Feint of the Cut-over, I parry Counter-Quarte, deceive into the low line (*en main seconde*), lunge	Cut-over and counter-disengage into the low line	Counter-Quarte, Septime.

Parries to meet these Attacks and Simple and Compound Ripostes.

ATTACKS.

Analysed.	Without Analysis.	PARRIES.
I open the line—Feint of the direct thrust, I parry Quarte and Sixte, deceive, lunge	Feint of the direct thrust, One-Two	Quarte, Sixte, Quarte (or Counter-Sixte).
—Feint of the direct thrust, I parry Sixte and Quarte, deceive into the low line, lunge	Feint of the direct thrust, One-Two into the low line	Sixte, Quarte, Septime.
—Feint of the direct thrust ; I parry Quarte and Counter-Quarte, deceive, lunge	Feint of the direct thrust, double	Quarte, Counter-Quarte, Sixte (Counter Quarte).
—Feint of the direct thrust : I parry Quarte and Counter-Quarte, deceive into the low line, lunge	Feint of the direct thrust, double into the low line	Quarte, Counter-Carte, Septime.
—Feint of the direct thrust, I parry Quarte and Septime, deceive, lunge	Feint of the direct thrust, feint low, disengage high	Quarte, Septime, Quarte.
—Feint of the direct thrust, I parry Quarte and Septime, deceive into the low line, lunge	Feint of the direct thrust, feint low, disengage low	Quarte, Septime, Octave (or Counter-Septime),
—Feint of the direct thrust, I parry Counter-Sixte, Quarte, deceive, lunge	Feint of the direct thrust, counter disengage, disengage	Counter - Sixte, Quarte, Sixte (or Counter-Quarte).

ATTACKS		PARRIES.
Analysed.	*Without Analysis.*	
—Feint of the direct thrust, I parry Counter-Sixte, Quarte, deceive into the low line, lunge	Feint of the direct thrust, counter - disengage, disengage low	Sixte Counter - Sixte, Quarte, Septime.
—Feint of the direct thrust, I parry twice Counter-Quarte, deceive, lunge	Feint of the direct thrust, counter - disengage twice	Twice Counter - Quarte, Sixte, (thrice Counter-Quarte).
—Feint of the direct thrust, I parry twice Counter-Quarte, deceive into the low line, lunge	Feint of the direct thrust, counter - disengage, counter-disengage low	Twice Counter - Quarte, Septime.
—Feint of the direct thrust, I parry Counter-Quarte, Septime, deceive into the high line, lunge	Feint of the direct thrust, counter-disengage below, disengage high	Counter-Quarte, Septime, Quarte.
—Feint of the direct thrust, I parry Counter-Quarte, Septime, deceive in the low line, lunge	Feint of the direct-thrust, counter-disengage low, disengage low	Counter-Quarte, Septime, Octave (or Counter-Septime).
Feint of disengagement, I parry Quarte and Sixte, deceive, lunge	One-Two-Three	Quarte, Sixte, Quarte (or Counter-Sixte).
Feint of disengagement, I parry Sixte and Quarte, deceive in low line, lunge	One-Two-Three low line	Sixte, Quarte, Septime.
Feint of disengagement, I parry Quarte, Counter-Quarte, deceive, lunge	One - Two counter - disengage	Quarte, Counter-Quarte, Sixte (or Counter-Quarte).

	ATTACKS.		PARRIES.
	Analysed.	*Without Analysis.*	
	Feint of disengagement, I parry Quarte, Counter-Quarte, deceive into low line, lunge	One - Two - counter-disengage low	Quarte, Counter-Quarte, Septime.
	Feint of disengagement, I parry Quarte and Septime, deceive into high line, lunge	Feint of disengagement, feint low, disengage high	Quarte, Septime, Quarte.
	Feint of disengagement, I parry Quarte and Septime, deceive into low line, lunge	Feint of disengagement, feint low, disengage low	Quarte-Septime, Octave (or Counter-Septime).
	Feint of disengagement, I parry Counter-Sixte, Quarte, deceive, lunge	Double and disengage	Counter-Sixte, Quarte, Sixte (or Counter-Quarte).
	Feint of disengagement, I parry Counter-Sixte, Quarte, deceive into low line, lunge	Double and disengage low	Counter - Sixte, Quarte, Septime.
	Feint of disengagement, I parry twice Counter-Quarte, deceive, lunge	Treble disengagement	Twice Counter - Quarte, Sixte, (thrice Counter-Quarte).
	Feint of disengagement, I parry twice Counter-Quarte, deceive into low line, lunge	Treble disengagement into low line	Twice Counter-Quarte, Septime.
	Feint of disengagement, I parry Counter-Quarte, Septime deceive into high line, lunge	Feint of double into low line, disengage high	Counter-Quarte, Septime, Quarte.

ATTACKS.		PARRIES.
Analysed.	*Without Analysis.*	
Feint of disengagement, I parry Counter-Quarte, Septime, deceive into low line, lunge	Feint of double into low line, disengage low	Counter-Quarte, Septime, Octave (or Counter-Septime).
Feint of disengagement, I parry Septime, Quarte, deceive, lunge	Feint of disengagement low, One-Two, high	Septime, Quarte, Sixte (or Counter-Quarte)
Feint of disengagement, I parry Septime, Quarte, deceive, low lunge	Feint of disengagement low, feint high, disengage low	Septime, Quarte, Septime.
Feint of disengagement, I parry Septime, Octave, deceive high, lunge	Feint of disengagement low, feint low, disengage high	Septime, Octave, Sixte.
Feint of disengagement, I parry Septime, Octave, deceive low, lunge	Feint of disengagement low, feint low, disengage low	Septime, Octave, Septime (or Counter-Octave).
Feint of disengagement, I parry Septime, Counter-Septime, deceive into high line, lunge	Feint of disengagement low, disengage low, counter-disengage, high	Septime, Counter-Septime, Quarte.
Fent of disengagement, I parry Septime, Counter-Septime, deceive low, lunge	Feint of disengagement low, feint low, counter-disengage low	Septime, Counter-Septime, Octave (or twice Counter-Septime).

Attacks on the Blade.

Beat—Pressure—Froissement.

This series consists of the movements enumerated in
the Second, Third and Fourth Series, preceded by the
beat, pressure and froissement, the instructor announcing
his commands accordingly.

The **Change of Engagement** and the **Double
Engagement** for the above purpose may be included in
" attacks on the blade." Further, they may be joined
with attacks on the blade. For example, " Change-
beat, disengage," " Double change pressure, one-two,"
etc., the attack on the blade completing the single or
double change.

*Parries to meet the above Attacks with Simple and
Compound Ripostes.*

(See parries of the Second, Third and Fourth Series.)

Prise de fer (Taking of the Blade).

By Opposition, The Bind, Croisé, Envelopment.

These movements may precede the Second, Third and
Fourth Series, the instructor announcing his commands
accordingly.

Examples.

Analysed.	Without Analysis.
On my extended arm— oppose—straighten the arm—lunge.	Oppose, lunge.
On my extended arm— change oppose—straighten the arm—lunge.	Change, **oppose**, lunge.
On my extended arm— bind in straightening the arm—lunge.	Bind.

Examples.

Analysed.	*Without Analysis.*
On my disengagement—parry Counter-Quarte and riposte by the " croisé."	Counter-Quarte, croisé.
On my extended arm—envelop—lunge.	Envelop.

Etc., etc.

Parries to meet the above Attacks with Simple or Compound Ripostes.

Extend the arm ; I oppose and lunge—parry Sixte (Counter-Quarte)—riposte direct or in the low line from Sixte ; by disengagement from Counter-Quarte.

Extend the arm ; I oppose in changing the engagement and lunge—parry Quarte (Counter-Sixte), etc.

Extend the arm ; I bind and lunge—parry Octave, etc.

Extend the arm ; I envelop and lunge—parry Quarte (Counter-Sixte).

Etc., etc.

SEVENTH SERIES : ATTACKS ON THE OPPOSING PREPARATION.

Various Preparations.

The Advance—Attacks on the Blade—Prise de fer.

The attacks of the Second and Third Series may be operated against these various preparations.

Examples.

On my advance—the stop-thrust (from immobility or in lunging).

On my beat—deceive in disengaging.

On my change of engagement—deceive in disengaging.

On my double change—deceive the second change in disengaging.

On my feint—beat (pressure, froissement).

Etc., etc.

44

Parries to meet the above Attacks and Simple or Compound Ripostes.

Advance—I make the stop-thrust—parry Sixte (Counter Quarte)—riposte direct.

Beat—I deceive in disengaging—parry Counter-Quarte (Sixte) and riposte by disengagement (from Counter Quarte) in the low line (from Sixte).

Change the engagement—I deceive in disengaging— parry Counter-Sixte (Quarte) and riposte by the cut-over (from Counter-Sixte), by the cut-over into the low line *en main seconde* (from Quarte).

Double change—I deceive on the second change in disengaging—parry Counter-Quarte (Sixte) and riposte by the cut-over (from Counter-Quarte), by One-two (from Sixte).

Extend the arm—I make a beat and lunge—parry Quarte (Counter-Sixte), etc.

Etc., etc.

EIGHTH SERIES : COUNTER-RIPOSTES.

Simple Counter-Ripostes on Simple Ripostes.

Examples.

Feint of disengagement—I parry Sixte and lunge— parry Sixte (Counter-Quarte) and counter-riposte direct.

Disengage—I parry Counter-Quarte and riposte direct— parry Quarte (Counter-Sixte) and counter-riposte direct.

Etc., etc.

Simple Counter-Ripostes on Compound Ripostes.

Examples.

Feint of disengagement—I parry Counter-Quarte and disengage—parry, Sixte (counter-Quarte) and counter-riposte direct.

Feint of disengagement—I parry Sixte and riposte by One-Two—parry Quarte, Sixte (Counter-Quarte) and counter-riposte direct.

Disengage—I parry Sixte and disengage—parry Counter-Sixte and counter-riposte direct.

Etc., etc.

Compound Counter-Ripostes on Simple Ripostes (Compound).

Feint of disengagement—I parry Sixte and lunge—parry Sixte (Counter-Quarte) and counter-riposte by One-Two (from Sixte) by disengagement (from Counter-Quarte).

Disengage—I parry Sixte and riposte direct—parry counter-Quarte and counter-riposte by the double.
Etc., etc.

NINTH SERIES : COUNTER-ATTACKS AND VARIETIES OF ATTACK.

Counter - attacks—The Redouble—The Reprise—Remise—Counter—Time.

Examples.

Counter-attacks.

I advance—stop-thrust (from immobility, half or full lunge).

I make One-Two from Sixte—time-thrust in Sixte.

I disengage from Quarte-tension.
Etc., etc.

The Redouble.

Disengage—I parry Counter-Quarte in retiring—bring the left foot up and lunge again with disengagement.

Disengage—I parry Sixte—return to guard and redouble by disengagement.
Etc., etc.

Remise.

Disengage—I parry Counter-Quarte and riposte by disengagement—Remise with opposition in Sixte.

Disengage—I parry Sixte and riposte by One-Two—Remise on my absence of blade (on feint)
Etc., etc.

Reprise.

Disengage—I parry Counter-Quarte without riposting—renew attack in low line (*en main seconde*).

Disengage—I parry Sixte without riposting—renew attack by disengagement.
Etc., etc.

Counter-time.

Advance—on my stop-thrust parry Quarte and lunge.
Etc., etc.

CONCLUSION OF FOIL SECTION.

PART TWO

SECTION THREE

Épée Fencing

Principal Characteristics of the Épée.

78. The principles governing the tactics of foil-fencing outlined in Chapter III of Section II apply generally to those of épée-play. Certain factors, however, must not be ignored. One must not overlook the **element of chance,** the frequent absence of an opposing defensive instinct, and the unsatisfactory possibility of a double hit. What **should** happen with the foil may not occur with the épée, and unless the foilist approaches his task with the épée in a prudent spirit he may court disaster.

The fundamental difference between the épée and the foil bout lies in the suppression of all convention.

With the épée, which represents the French duelling sword, hits are valid on any part of the body. This imposes at once an obligation on the parties to place themselves out of lunging distance.

The larger target naturally offers a wider scope to the attacker and decreases at the same time the defensive value of the parry, which may in certain cases uncover and expose the sword-hand or arm.

On the other hand, the aggressor with his greater field of activity offers an extended target to the counter-thrust.

The greatest danger to the épéeist comes from the possibility of being counter-attacked, by an opponent masterly in his direction of the point, at those parts of the target which are most advanced from the body (the sword-hand, arm, shoulder, mask).

Thus, even the simplest of offensive movements cannot be guaranteed the security that would be enjoyed with the foil.

It is the proportion of hits given and received with the foil that decides the superiority of one party over another and while this difference usually proclaims a greater intrinsic fencing merit such a consideration need not necessarily affect the épéeist although any degree of artistry he employs is to be highly commended. As a " duellist " his paramount object is to hit and not be hit—in other words, to score and in doing so emerge unscathed. That is the one inexorable rule of the épée.

The épéeist should therefore wage his battle in the spirit of the duel, where each hit on either side may cause disability or death. It is as if he were fencing with the mask off. Thus, without cramping his initiative, he must be patient, avoid rashness and disdain all unnecessary risks. Legislation has adversely affected the character of this weapon by extending competition bouts beyond the one vital hit and the épéeist is consequently constrained to prolong the exercise of his imagination.

In brief, the principal characteristics of the épée combat are :—

> Augmentation and constant change of the distance between the opponents.
>
> The risk attending the offensive not met by the positive defence ; and
>
> The added advantage of counter-point tactics.

Principal Tactics.

79. From the foregoing considerations emanate the following directions which supplement those already outlined for the foil. They complete the education of the exponent of the épée, a sound knowledge of the grammar of fencing as provided by the use of the foil and its adaptation to the special tactics demanded of the épée, the practical arm.

(a) Combine as often as possible all attacks with the advance and all defensive actions with the retreat.

(b) Unless you have an exceptionally good reason, do not directly attack the body without first making some preparation such as the *prise de fer*.

(*c*) Fetter to disturb your opponent at the outset by prudent attacks at the sword-hand and arm. In this way you gain the distance for a more conclusive onslaught ; alternatively your feint of attack at the body may bring about exposure of the advanced parts (swordhand and arm).

(*d*) Employ as frequently as possible the counterattack (the time and stop thrusts), otherwise counterthrusting tactics, assuring a constant and severe point in line.

Hints to the Instructor.

80. (*a*) **Develop** to the highest degree **the judgment and idea of distance.**

(*b*) **Combine** as often as possible **attack and parry** with the **advance** and **retreat** respectively.

(*c*) Teach the pupil to attack at the **advanced parts** (the sword-hand and arm), employing the exercises already prescribed for foil attacks, eliminating for obvious reasons the **cut-over.**

(*d*) Teach him to defend the **advanced parts** by the necessary displacement of the hand and shell-guard from the threatened quarter, the point being directed towards the opposing sword-arm, and by counterattacking the sword-arm with the cover described above.

In **defending the lower part of the trunk and leg** make him bring the right foot to the left while counterattacking in the high line. Secondly, make him parry **Seconde,** riposting in the high line.

(*e*) In **attacking the body** it is preferable first to assail the **advanced parts** either by the **half** or **full Lunge,** then follow with the **Redouble** by bringing the left foot towards the right, or by the full lunge as the case may be.

(*f*) Familiarize the pupil with attacks by the **Prise de fer.** Encourage a frequent use of these movements and—of equal importance—teach him to evade by the **Derobement** those his opponent would execute upon him.

To avoid the opposing **Derobement,** the pupil is recommended to precede his **Prise de fer** by a **Pressure, Beat** or **Engagement.**

(*g*) **Develop his strength of hand.** Attacks on the blade and *prises de fer* being of major importance with this weapon, demand a full authority in their execution.

49

(*h*) The parry of **Prime** which uncovers the whole of the forearm is excluded from this instruction, but the low parry deflecting the point downwards and diagonally, known as **Quinte,** may be used. **Seconde** and its **Counter** are to be preferred to **Octave** and **Counter-Octave.**

(*i*) Practise as frequently as possible the **Counter-attacks** (time and stop thrust). The defender may successfully meet the opposing attack at the body by a time or stop thrust at the sword-hand or arm. If the impetus of the attack be considered, it is wise to combine the counter-thrust with the **Retreat.**

(*j*) Exercise your pupil thoroughly in the parrying of these counter-attacks.

81. The movements and the different offensive and defensive actions indicated under Sections I and II of the foil code are applicable to épée fencing save in the following cases :—

Position of " On Guard "—Assuming ' On Guard "
Position (Section I, Chapter I, Article II).

(10) Instead of (3) . . . the point of the weapon at shoulder level . . . (Fig. 5), the fencer will hold his blade as a prolongation of the forearm, the latter being horizontal (Fig. 26).

FIG. 26.

Assuming " On Guard " Position.—See (11)

Series of Exercises.

(Analysed, then without Analysis.)

Assuming the " On Guard " position in five movements:
Extend the arm.
Lunge.
Return to Guard.
Advance.
Retreat.
Retreat in bringing right foot to left.
Fencing positions : Sixte, Quarte, Seconde and Tierce.
Reassemble.
Salute.

SECOND SERIES : SIMPLE ATTACKS AT THE ADVANCED PARTS.

Examples.

(1) Without Lunging.

On my extended arm, point high (low)—point at the hand underneath (above).

On my extended arm, point high (low)--point at the forearm underneath (above).

On my invitation in Quarte—point at the outside of the hand.

On my invitation in Quarte—point at the outside of the forearm.

On my invitation in Sixte— point at the inside of the hand.

On my invitation in Sixte—point at the inside of the forearm.

The Instructor will make the appropriate exposure thus : greater for the sword-hand, lesser for the arm.

(2) In Advancing.

On my extended arm, point high (low)—point at the hand underneath (above) on the advance.
Etc., etc., as above.

(3) In Lunging.

On my guard, point high (low)—extend at the hand underneath (above)—lunge.
Etc., etc., as above.

(4) In Advancing and Lunging.

On my guard, point high (low)—feint at the hand underneath (above) on the advance—lunge.

Etc., etc., as above.

Counter-attacks on Simple Attacks at the Advanced Parts.

Examples.

(1) On Guard point high (low)—I point at the hand
below (above)—Extend at the hand (the arm) above
(below).

(2) On Guard point high (low)—I point at the forearm
below (above)—Extend at the hand (arm) above
(below).

(3) On Guard point high (low)—I point at the hand
below (above) in advancing—Stop-thrust at the hand
(arm) in retreating.

(4) On Guard point high (low)—I point at the forearm
below (above) in advancing—Stop-thrust at the hand
(arm) in retreating.

(5) On Guard point high (low)—I lunge at the hand
below (above)—Extend at the hand (arm) above
(below) in retreating.

(6) On Guard point high (low)—I lunge at the forearm
below (above)—Extend at the hand (arm) above
(below) in retreating.

(7) On Guard point high (low)—I advance and lunge at
the hand below (above)—Stop-thrust at the hand (arm)
above (below) in retreating.

(8) On Guard point high (low)—I advance and lunge at
the forearm below (above)—Stop-thrust at the hand
(arm) above (below) in retreating.

THIRD SERIES : ATTACKS AT THE ADVANCED PARTS PRECEDED BY ATTACKS ON THE BLADE.

Pressure—Beat—Froissement.

Examples.

(1) Without Lunging.

On my extended arm, point high—press—point at the
hand below.

Etc., etc.

(2) **In Advancing.**

On my guard, point low—beat—point at the forearm
above in advancing.

Etc., etc.

(3) **In Lunging.**

On my extended arm, point high—*froissez*—point at
the outside of sword-arm—lunge.

Beat—extend at the outside of sword-hand—lunge.

Etc., etc.

*Counter-attacks on Attacks at the Advanced Parts
preceded by Attacks on the Blade.*

These are indicated in Counter-attacks on Simple
Attacks at the Advanced Parts (Second Series).

FOURTH SERIES : ATTACKS TO THE BODY PRECEDED
BY ATTACKS TO THE ADVANCED PARTS.

The pupil will make the attack at the advanced part
(hand or arm), the instructor counter-attacking at the
hand or arm ; the pupil thrusts at the body after
finding the blade.

Examples.

(1) Thrust at the hand (forearm) above (below)— I
counter-attack at the arm—beat, lunge at the body.

(2) Thrust at the hand (forearm) above (below) on the
advance—I counter-attack at the arm above—beat,
lunge at the body.

(3) On my guard, point high (low)—press (beat) and
thrust at the hand below (above)—I counter attack
at the arm above (below)—beat, lunge at the body.

(4) Same exercises, the attack at the advanced parts
being preceded by an advance.

(5) Same exercises, the attack at the advanced parts
being preceded by a half-lunge.

The half-lunge may be followed by a complete lunge
or by a *reprise* of the guard to the fore preceding the
lunge.

Parries of these Attacks.

The Instructor executes the movements prescribed
for the pupil in the above exercises, the pupil parrying
the final attack at the body by Seconde, Quarte, Sixte
and, principally, by their counters.

To facilitate the various *prises de fer* the Instructor will
cause the movements to be made at first on his extended
arm.

Examples.

(1) On my extended arm—Oppose in Tierce—lunge.

   On my extended arm—Oppose in Tierce on the ad
   vance—lunge.

(2) On my extended arm—Oppose in Quarte—lunge.

   On my extended arm—Oppose in Quarte on the advance—lunge.

(3) On my extended arm—Envelop in Sixte—lunge.

   On my extended arm—Envelop in Sixte on the advance—lunge.

(4) On my extended arm—Bind in Seconde—lunge.

   On my extended arm—Bind in Seconde on the advance—lunge.

(5) Advance—I make the stop-thrust—Oppose (change
   oppose)—lunge.

(6) Advance—I stop-thrust—Oppose with Tierce (Quarte
   or Seconde)—lunge.
   Etc., etc.

The above movements then to be executed on the
Instructor's partially extended arm, the *prise de fer*
being preceded by a beat or pressure in the opposite line.

Parries (or Derobements) of the Prises de Fer.

The Instructor will place the pupil with extended or
partially extended arm or make him execute the stop-
thrust, then he will cause him to parry or make the
derobement with or without the retreat.

(1) Extend the arm—I attack with the *prise de fer* in Tierce—parry Counter-Quarte and riposte.

(2) Extend the arm—I attack with *prise de fer* in Quarte—parry Counter-Sixte and riposte in low line.

(3) Extend the arm—I attack in binding in Seconde, deceive in the high line on the retreat.

(4) Extend the arm—I attack by a pressure in Quarte and a *prise de fer* in Tierce—parry Counter-Quarte and riposte.

(5) I advance—Stop-thrust—I attack on the advance with *prise de fer* in Seconde—deceive in the high line on the retreat.

(6) I advance—Stop-thrust—I parry Counter-Quarte and lunge—parry Counter-Sixte and riposte direct (low).

(7) I advance—Stop-thrust—I attack by a pressure in Quarte and a *prise de fer* in Tierce—Parry Counter-Quarte and riposte.

Etc., etc.

SIXTH SERIES : RENEWED " PRISES DE FER."

Examples.

(1) On my extended arm (half-extended)—Bind from Quarte to Seconde on the advance—I deceive into the high line—Oppose in Tierce (Sixte) and lunge to the body.

(2) On my extended arm (half-extended)—Oppose in Tierce (Sixte) on the advance—I deceive into the low line—oppose in Seconde and lunge to the body.

(3) On my extended arm (half-extended)—Bind from Quarte to Seconde on the advance—I deceive into the high line—bind from Quarte to Seconde and lunge to the body.

(4) On my extended arm (half-extended) —Bind from Quarte to Seconde on the advance—I deceive into the high line—Bind from Tierce (Sixte) to Septime and lunge to the body.

(5) On my extended arm (half-extended)—Bind from Quarte to Seconde on the advance—I deceive into the high line—oppose in Tierce (Sixte) and lunge to the body.

(6) On my extended arm (half-extended)—Oppose in Tierce on the advance—I deceive into the high line—change oppose in Tierce (Sixte)—I deceive into the low line—oppose in Seconde and lunge to the body.

(7) On my extended arm (half-extended)—Oppose in Tierce (Sixte) on the advance—I deceive into the low line—oppose in Seconde—I deceive into the high line—Bind from Quarte to Seconde and lunge to the body.

(8) On my extended arm (half-extended)—Oppose in Tierce on the advance—I deceive into the low line—oppose in Seconde—I deceive into the high line—bind from Tierce (Sixte) to Septime and lunge to the body.

Each of the above exercises may also be carried out with the Instructor retreating and deceiving the first " prise," the pupil combining the last with the attack on the advance.

Parries of Renewed " Prises " and " Derobements."

The Instructor executing the various " prises " will exercise the pupil in deceiving them from immobility and then on the retreat. Further, he should be taught to parry the final " prises " which terminate in the high line and for preference to deceive those finishing in the low line.

Examples.

(1) On my *prises de fer* in Seconde, Seconde, Tierce (see example No. 5 of renewed " prises ") on the advance—deceive twice into the high line and parry my final in Tierce by Counter-Quarte.

(2) On my *prises de fer* in Tierce, Tierce Seconde (see example 6) on the advance—deceive three times on the retreat.

(3) On my *prises de fer* in Tierce, Seconde, Seconde (see example No. 7) and on my lunge—deceive three times from immobility.

CONCLUSION OF ÉPÉE SECTION.

56

PART THREE

SECTION FOUR

Sabre Fencing

Principal Tactics.

82. The Sabre is an attractive and, by reason of its dual function (point and edge), spectacular weapon.

It possesses a wider convention than that of the foil in that **the target is composed of the whole of the body above the hips including the arms and similarly certain rights exercised by the foilist are fully respected**—*i.e.*, **a direct riposte is rightly given precedence over a remise in the case of simultaneous hits, etc. Thus, unlike the épée, only one principal may profit from a double hit.**

The exposure—particularly to the edge—of the advanced parts deprives the weapon of much of its positive character while investing it with the duelling potentialities of the épée though without the latter's conclusive effects.

It will be appreciated, therefore, that the principal tactics outlined under Sections II and III for the foil and sabre may be readily applied in the main and wherever appropriate to the sabre bout. The dual properties possessed by the sabre (point and edge), however, raise points for special consideration.

(a) Give a slight preference to the **point over the edge in attack.** It is a more decisive factor, calls for greater resolution in the parry, and is much less susceptible to the time cut at arm. It should be preceded more often than not by an attack on the blade by a beat or *prise de fer*, especially in " Third " of " Fourth " (see fencing positions).

(b) Remember that the sabre-arm is always a fruitful source of your opponent's inspiration. **Do not neglect to keep it constantly under cover and out of danger.**

(c) As with the épée, the larger target offers increased facilities to the attacker while placing a greater onus on the defence by the parry, therefore seize every opportunity to profit by the attacker's exposure of his arm by a stop-cut and do not hesitate to employ the stop and time-thrust frequently.

(*d*) Again, as the versatility of the sabre provides increased scoring possibilities, especially at close range, it demands extreme mobility. **As often as possible employ the Italian method of attacking on the advance known as the "Attacco di Balestra" and the retreat by the "Salto in dietro" (the backward spring).** These movements are explained hereunder. They are equally applicable to foil and épée fencing.

The "Balestra" Attack.

83. With the body erect in order to depart from complete immobility, raise the right foot forward and take a short jump off the left, alighting a short pace forward, **both feet touching the floor simultaneously.** Follow with the lunge.

Observation.—The whole action in a direct attack or of one feint will be completed without a break. In a more complicated offensive the length of the pause will naturally depend upon the number of feints employed. This staccato movement forms an excellent prelude to counter-time strategy.

Note.—The descent on the right foot should be made on the flat or ball of the foot to avoid jarring the heel.

The Backward Spring.

84. (*a*) From the "On Guard" position, bend the legs well to obtain the maximum spring. Keep the trunk erect and impose the weight of the body on the left leg. Bring the right leg up to the left, transferring the weight to the right foot, simultaneously lifting the left. From the pressure of the right foot jump back on to the left leg, which again bears the weight of the body. Plant the right foot down and resume normal poise and stance.

(*b*) From the lunge, press with the right heel, at the same time bending the left leg. Keeping the latter well bent, bring the right to the left and continue as from the "On Guard" position.

Observation.—The backward spring enables the sabreur to break off the exchanges with safety and/or to withdraw to recover.

Note.—The time or stop cut at arm in particular should invariably be accompanied by the backward spring. It is a natural and logical step emphasising the movement and clarifying the margin of time.

Movements prescribed for foil and épée under Sections I and II are applicable in the main to the sabre, save in the following instances :—

The Grip.

(Section I, Chapter I, Article I.)

8. . . . There is little difference between the grip of the foil and épée and that of the sabre. In the latter case the fingers bring the handle into final contact with the heel or ball of the hand. The thumb, first and little fingers are the main controlling members. (See Fig. 2.)

The Position of the Guard.

(Article II.)

10. (1) Place the feet at right angles, the heels touching, the left foot perpendicular to the line of the fencers ; the legs stretched without stiffness, the body erect, shoulders level and relaxed. **From a fully extended arm with the hand in pronation and keeping the left hand resting lightly ˙on the hip, bring back forearm and sabre directly until both diagonally cross the chest, the blade touching the left hip, a straight line from elbow to point being maintained throughout** (Fig. 27).

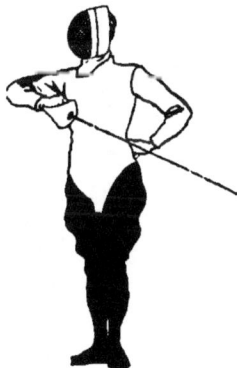

FIG 27.

59

(2) **Return** sabre and forearm directly by a .semi-circular motion to the " point in line " position (arm extended, hand in pronation, describing a straight line from shoulder to point) (Fig. 28).

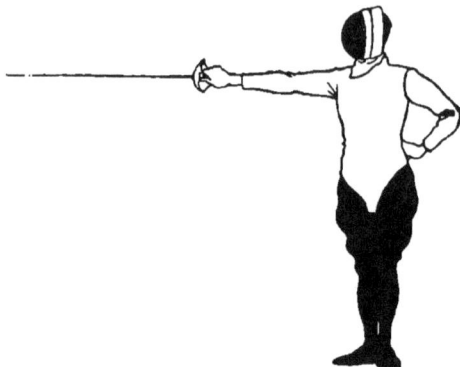

FIG. 28.

(3) Bend the legs without moving the feet (maintaining the trunk erect), at the same time flexing the right arm, the elbow free from the body and in a straight line with the point, the hand on a level with the shoulder (Fig. 29).

FIG. 29.

(4) Advance the right foot and place it flat opposite the left heel at a distance suitable to the height (Fig. 30).

FIG. 30.

(See also 11—Forming " On Guard " to the rear.)

Fencing Positions of the Sabre.

(Section I—Chapter II—Article I.)

24. These are six in number—**Prima** (Prime, First), **Seconda** (Seconde, Second), **Terza** (Tierce, Third). **Quarta** (Quarte, Fourth), **Quinta** (Quinte, Fifth) and **Sesta** (Sixte, Sixth).

Prima, Seconda and Quinta (all in pronation) are classified as **Primary Parries**, Terza (pronation), Quarta and Sesta (both supination) are of secondary category. They are described and illustrated as follows :—

25. **Prima** (pronation).—Protecting the chest and left cheek. Forearm and sabre forming a straight line,

point inclined downwards and slightly to the left ; **cutting** edge upwards (Figs. 31 and 32).

Fig. 31. Fig. 32.

26. **Seconda** (pronation). — Protecting the right flank. Point inclined downwards from the wrist, cutting edge practically lateral (Figs. 33 and 34).

Fig. 33. Fig. 34.

27. **Terza** (pronation).—Protecting right cheek ; forearm and sabre forming a straight line, point inclined upwards ; cutting edge lateral (Figs. 35 and 36).

FIG. 35.   FIG. 36.

28. **Quarta** (supination).—Protecting the chest. Sabre almost at right angles to the forearm, point upwards and inclined to the left ; cutting edge diagonal to the line of the adversary (Figs. 37 and 38).

FIG. 37.   FIG. 38.

29. **Quinta** (pronation).—Protecting the head. Forearm and sabre forming a straight line horizontally, point inclined towards the left ; cutting edge upwards (Figs. 39 and 40).

FIG. 39.   FIG. 40.

30. **Sesta** (supination).—Protecting the head. Sabre almost at right angles to the forearm, blade practically horizontal, point inclined towards the right cutting edge upwards (Figs. 41 and 42).

FIG. 41.   FIG. 42.

The positions of Terza and Seconda are the best to employ as they offer respectively fuller protection to the hand and arm.

31. **Terza Bassa** (Low Third—pronation).—Protecting right flank. Elbow in contact with the flank, point directed upwards and to the right, cutting edge diagonal to the line of the opponent. (Figs. 43 and 44.)

FIG. 43.   FIG. 44.

32. **Quarta Bassa** (Low Fourth—supination).—Protecting the chest. Forearm in contact with the right hip, point directed upwards and to the left, cutting edge diagonal to the line of the opponent (Figs. 45 and 46.)

FIG. 45.   FIG. 46.

The Engagement.

33. In the engagements for sabre-fencing, contact is effected by edge to edge.

Sabre in Hand.

(*Sciabola in Mano.*)

The " Molinello."

85. The greatest enjoyment and satisfaction can only be derived from the art of sabre fencing by the maximum development of the sense of touch and by the fullest observance of the cardinal and fundamental principle governing the correct manipulation of the cutting weapon—**Sabre in hand.**

Sabre in hand means controlled and conserved strength. It means the elimination of force and the ability to check the edge on impact with the objective.

To acquire this sense of touch and to fence with **sabre in hand** it is necessary to develop the strength of the wrist and fingers and to render the arm—as distinct from the former—as supple as possible so that it may act with the utmost freedom of motion. The practice of the circular cut known as the " Molinello " is an invaluable adjunct in this respect.

This circular cut is a movement by which blade forearm and point describe a complete circle or part thereof in their path to the objective. " Molinelli " may be horizontal, diagonal or vertical, and may be performed from immobility or combined with the lunge.

For the purposes explained above the last-named " Molinello " is recommended as sufficient to produce and maintain suppleness, speed of arm, lightness of touch, and stamina.

The particular " Molinello " advised is the circular cut at head from Second and is executed as follows :—

From the position of Second (see Figs. 33 and 34) slightly rotate the arm inwards until the position of First is reached (see Figs. 31 and 32). Now withdraw sabre and forearm in a downward sweep, keeping the elbow and upper arm completely still. Continue this circular path until forearm and sabre are parallel with the shoulders and the cutting edge is directly upwards.

From this position complete the circling movement to the head with the lunge, the cut finishing in a straight line from shoulder to point. The entire evolution should be made without pause. Recover by returning sabre and forearm by the same circular route to Second.

The exercise should be carried out with punctilious care, the student seeking to make contact with the same degree of touch throughout. The lesson should be frequently preceded, especially in the earlier stages, by a series of the "Molinello" from immobility and concluded with the addition of the lunge. In the former case ten to twenty of these movements should be sufficient to ensure the necessary free functioning of the sabrearm. The number of "Molinelli" executed with the lunge should be steadily increased with the development of the pupil's stamina until a hundred of these evolutions may be performed without undue fatigue.

Offensive Actions.

(Section II—Chapter I—Article I.)

86. Point or Edge may be used with the sabre.

The Thrust.

The thrust is executed with the hand in pronation, in **Third** or **Second** according to the prescriptions laid down under Article III of Chapter I of Section I (The Development).

The Cut.

The Cut is delivered by carrying the sabre below or above the opposing arm (cut-over or disengagement) to the objective. The lunge should be synchronized with the straightening of the arm and the grip compressed on touching to produce a resilient contact as distinct from a "lay-on." In the case of an indirect attack the arm will for the greater part, be already straightened for the feint, and this extension should be maintained as far as possible to the final delivery.

Cutting strokes are directed as follows :—To the right flank, the right cheek, the head, and the chest.

They are executed in the following manner :—

The Cut at Flank.—From Third—Lower the point in a progressive movement simultaneously with the lunge. Compress grip on contact, the attack finishing in a straight line from shoulder to point.

The Cut at Cheek.—From Second—Raise the point in a progressive movement simultaneously with the lunge. Compress grip on contact, the attack finishing in a straight line from shoulder to point.

The Cut at Head.—From Second (see " Molinello "). From Third—Retain the hand in pronation and raise the blade along the edge of the opposing sabre until the point is reached, then impart a half rotation to the arm so that the edge is facing downwards. Simultaneously straighten the arm and lunge. Compress grip on contact, the attack finishing in a straight line from shoulder to point. (See the Cut-over, Section II, Chapter I, Article I, para. No. 40.)

The Cut or Slice at Chest.—From Third—Retain the hand in pronation and raise the blade along the edge of the opposing sabre (as in the first part of the cut-over) until the point is reached. Half rotate the arm and extend directly to the chest so that the blade arrives **flat** simultaneously with the lunge. **Convert to a cut** by withdrawing the blade across the chest, turning into supination—*i.e.*, towards the position of Fourth. Simultaneously return to Guard, resuming the Third position.

Observation.—An attack with the edge from Third or Second at the adversary's inside line (his left side) inevitably involves an external motion of the arm. For the purpose of a direct attack the above method reduces the rotation rendering the movement swifter, and less ostentatious.

The circular cut at chest is parried by First or Fourth and leaves the attacker in a disadvantageous position with regard to his defence against his opponent's riposte **unless the circular movement be continued after the blade has been met** when it will but check its impetus, permitting it to fly readily to Fourth, Third or Fifth as the case may be. Thus the attacker must **always** " draw through " when making this particular **stroke.**

Note.—It will be seen that these attacks are launched from Third and/or Second. **These are the positions to be adopted throughout,** as they offer the greatest protection to the sabre-arm and hand. Fourth, as a rest position out of distance may also be affected and may occasionally be adapted as a base for these direct attacks—viz., the cut at flank, the cut at cheek, the cut at head, and the cut at chest.

68

Defensive Actions.

(Section II—Chapter II.)

All parries are executed with the edge and with the *forte* of the blade, and save in the case of Fourth, Low

FIG. 47.
FIRST PARRYING ATTACK AT CHEST

Fourth, Low Third, Second, and Sixth, should terminate in a straight line from elbow to point.

FIG. 48.
SECOND PARRYING ATTACK AT FLANK.

Such parries as Sixte, Septime and Octave lack the necessary stability and authority and should not be used with the cutting weapon.

FIG. 49.

THIRD PARRYING ATTACK AT CHEEK.

Those employed are—**First** (Prima) (Figs. 31 and 32), **Second** (Seconda) (Figs. 33 and 34), **Third** (Terza) (Figs. 35 and 36), **Low Third** Terza bassa) (Figs. 43

FIG. 50.

FOURTH PARRYING ATTACK WITH POINT.

and 44), **Fourth** (Quarta) (Figs. 37 and 38), **Low Fourth** (Quarta bassa) (Figs. 45 and 46), **Fifth** (Quinta) (Figs. 39 and 40), and **Sixth** (Sesta) (Figs. 41 and 42).

FIG. 51.

FIFTH PARRYING ATTACK AT HEAD.

FIG. 52.

SIXTH PARRYING ATTACK AT HEAD.

FIG. 53.

LOW THIRD PARRYING ATTACK AT FLANK.

FIG. 54.

LOW FOURTH PARRYING ATTACK AT CHEST.

Series of Exercises.

(With and without analysis.)

Assume the " On Guard " position in four movements.
Advance, Retreat.
Extend the arm.
Lunge.
Return to Guard.
Engage the blade (in Third).
Change the Engagement (to Second).
Fencing Positions (in numerical order and then other-
  wise). (Combine with advance and retreat.)
Reassemble (by bringing right foot to left and assuming
  standing position).
Salute.

SECOND SERIES : PRELIMINARY EXERCISES.

Molinelli (from Immobility and in Lunging).

(1) **Molinello at the head from immobility.**

On Guard in Second—Commence.

(2) **Riposte by Molinello at the head.**

On Guard in Second—I cut at chest—parry First
and riposte by Molinello at head.

(3) **Molinello at the head in lunging.**

On Guard in Second—Commence.

(4) **Molinello at the head in lunging from First.**

On Guard in Second—I cut at chest—parry First
and lunge with the Molinello.

When the student is sufficiently advanced the preliminary exercise No. 2 should be developed and prolonged, incorporating the Molinello and, so far as possible, circular ripostes, to the fourth or fifth counter-
riposte as follows :—

Examples.

(a) On Guard in Second—I cut at chest—parry First,
Molinello at the head ; I parry Fifth and reply at
chest—parry First, molinello at the head ; repeat
sequence ; I parry Sixth and riposte at flank ; parry
Second and riposte at chest.

(*b*) On Guard in Second—I cut at chest—parry First, Molinello at the head ; I parry Fifth and reply at chest—parry First, Molinello at the head ; repeat sequence ; I parry Sixth and riposte at flank—parry Second and riposte at cheek (low Third and riposte at chest).

(*c*) On Guard in Second—I cut at chest—parry First, Molinello at head ; I parry Fifth and reply at chest— parry First, Molinello at head ; I parry Sixth and riposte at flank ; parry Second and riposte at cheek ; I parry Third and riposte at head—parry Fifth and riposte at chest.

With variations, etc., etc., etc.

THIRD SERIES : SIMPLE ATTACKS.

(1) **Point Attacks.**

Analysed.	*Without Analysis.*
Direct Thrust by Graze (Foil) :	
On Guard in Third—Graze extend—lunge.	Graze, lunge.
On Guard in Second—Graze extend—lunge.	Graze, lunge.
Disengagement :	
On Guard in Third—Disengage and extend—lunge.	Disengage.
On Guard in Second—Disengage and extend—lunge.	Disengage.

(2) **Attacks with the Edge.**

On Guard in Third—Cut at flank.	Cut at flank.
On Guard in Fourth—Cutover and lunge at flank.	Cut at flank.
On Guard in Second—Cut at cheek.	Cut at cheek.
On Guard in Fourth—Cutover and lunge at cheek.	Cut at cheek.
On Guard in Third—Cutover and lunge at head.	Cut at head.
On Guard in Second—Molinello at the head.	Cut at head.

Analysed.	*Without Analysis.*
On Guard in Fourth—Cut at head.	Cut at head.
On Guard in Third—Cut-over and lunge at chest.	Cut at chest.
On Guard in Fourth—Cut at chest.	Cut at chest.

Parries to meet above Attacks and Simple Ripostes.

Examples.

On my graze in Third—oppose in Third—riposte at flank (head, chest, disengagement of point).

On my disengagement from Third—parry Fourth—riposte at cheek (head, chest, point).

On my disengagement from Third—parry First—riposte by Molinello at head (flank, chest, point).

On my disengagement from Third—parry Counter-Third—riposte at flank (head, chest, disengagement of point).

On my graze in Second—oppose in Second—riposte at cheek (graze point, disengagement of point).

On my disengagement from Second—parry Third—riposte at flank (head, chest, disengagement of point.)

On my disengagement from Second—parry Counter-Second—riposte at cheek (graze point, disengagement of point).

On my disengagement from Second—parry First—riposte by Molinello at head (flank, chest, point).

On my disengagement from Second—parry half-counter-Fourth—riposte at cheek (head, chest, point).

On my cut at flank from Third—parry Second—riposte at cheek, etc.

On my cut at cheek from Second—parry Third—riposte at flank, etc.

On my Molinello at head—parry Fifth—riposte at flank (chest, point).

On my cut at cheek from Fourth—parry Third—riposte at flank, etc.

On my cut at head from Third—parry Fifth—riposte at flank, etc.

On my cut at flank from Fourth—parry Second—riposte at cheek, etc.

On my cut at flank from Fourth—parry Low Third—riposte at head (graze point; flank, cheek).

On my cut at head from Third—parry Sixth—riposte at chest (flank).

On my cut at head from Fourth—parry Sixth—riposte at chest (flank).

On my Molinello at head—parry Sixth—riposte at chest (flank).

On my cut at chest from Third—parry Fourth—riposte at cheek, etc.

On my cut at chest from Third—parry First—riposte at head, etc.

Etc., etc.

FOURTH SERIES : ATTACKS COMPOSED OF ONE FEINT.

Examples.

Analysed.	*Without Analysis.*
On Guard in Third—-Feint of disengagement by point—I parry Fourth—deceive by passing under—cut at cheek.	Feint point, cut at cheek.
On Guard in Second—Feint of disengagement in high line—I parry Third—deceive and point.	One-Two with the point.
On Guard in Second—Feint of disengagement in high line—I parry half-counter-Fourth—deceive by passing under—cut at cheek.	Feint point, cut at cheek.
On Guard in Third—Feint at flank—I parry Second—deceive and cut at cheek.	Feint flank, cut at cheek.
On Guard in Second—Feint at cheek—I parry Third—deceive and cut at flank.	Feint cheek, cut at flank.
On Guard in Second—Feint at cheek—I parry Third—deceive and cut at chest.	Feint cheek, cut at chest.

76

Analysed.	*Without Analysis.*
On Guard in Second—Feint at cheek—I parry Third—deceive by disengagement of point.	Feint, cheek point.
On Guard in Second—Feint at head—I parry Fifth—deceive and point.	Feint head, point.
On Guard in Second—Feint at head—I parry Fifth—Cut at chest.	Feint head, cut at chest.
On Guard in Second—Feint at head—I parry Fifth—cut at flank.	Feint head, cut at flank.
On Guard in Third—Feint at chest by external rotation of bent arm—I parry First—cut at head.	Feint chest, cut at head.
On Guard in Third—Feint cut at chest (without rotation)—I parry Fourth—deceive by passing under—cut at cheek.	Feint cut at chest, cut at cheek.

Parries to meet above Attacks and Ripostes or Counter-attacks.

Examples.

On my feint point, cut at cheek—parry Fourth and Third—riposte or time-thrust.

On my One-Two with point—parry Third and Second—riposte.

On my One-Two with point—parry Third and Fourth—riposte.

On my feint point, cut at cheek from Second—Parry half - counter—Fourth and Third—riposte or time-thrust.

On my feint flank, cut at cheek—parry Second and Third—riposte or time-thrust.

On my feint cheek, cut at flank—parry Third and Second—riposte or time-thrust.

On my feint cheek, cut at chest—parry Third and Fourth (Low-Fourth)—riposte.

77

On my feint cheek, cut at chest—parry Third and First—riposte.

On my feint cheek, point—parry Third and Fourth (counter-Third)—riposte.

On my feint head, point—parry Fifth and Second (Fourth)—riposte.

On my feint head, cut at chest—parry Fifth and Fourth (First)—riposte.

On my feint head, cut at flank—parry Fifth and Second (Low Third)—riposte.

On my feint chest, cut at head—parry Fourth and Fifth—riposte.

On my feint cut at chest, cut at cheek—parry Fourth and Third—riposte.

FIFTH SERIES : ATTACKS COMPOSED OF TWO FEINTS AND THEIR PARRIES OR COUNTER-ATTACKS.

Examples.

Attacks.	*Defended by*
From Third, feint point, cheek, point.	Fourth, Third, Fourth (Counter-Third).
From Second, One-Two-three with point.	Third, Second, Third (half-counter-Fourth).
From Second, One-Two with point, cut at cheek.	Third, Second, Third.
From Third, feint flank, cheek, flank (disengagement with point)	Second, Third, Second (Fourth, or counter-attack in second time in Second).
From Second, feint cheek, flank, cheek.	Third, Second, Third (counter - attack in second time in Third).
From Second, feint cheek, point, cheek.	Third, Fourth, Third (counter - attack in second time in Third).
From Second, feint cheek, feint cut at chest, cheek.	Third, Fourth, Third (counter - attack in second time in Third).
From Second, feint head, point, cheek.	Fifth, Fourth (Second), Third.

Attacks.	*Defended by*
From Second, feint head, chest (external rotation), head.	Fifth, Fourth, Fifth.
From Second, feint head, feint cut at chest; cheek.	Fifth, Fourth, Third.
From Third, feint chest (external rotation), head, cut at chest.	Fourth, Fifth, Fourth.
From Third, feint chest (external rotation), head, flank.	Fourth, Fifth, Second (Low Third).
From Third, feint cut at chest, cheek, point.	Fourth, Third, Fourth (Second).
From Third, feint cut at chest, head, cut at chest.	Fourth, Fifth, Fourth.

Etc., etc.

Counter-attacks in Second and Third time ; counter-attacks are made in Second or Third. A time-thrust made on a two-feint attack after the deception of the first parry is known as a time-thrust in second time (Secondo Tempo). Delivered on a three-feint offensive after the second parry, it is called a time-thrust in third time (Terzo Tempo).

SIXTH SERIES : ATTACKS ON THE OPPOSING PREPARATION.

On the various preparations, attacks of the Third, Fourth and Fifth Series will be executed. These attacks themselves may be preceded by attacks on the blade, the " prise de fer " (*presa di ferro*) and combined with the " Balestra " movement and the retire by the backward spring.

Examples.

On my advance in Third—disengage with point (from immobility or with the lunge).

On my advance in Third—feint point, cut at cheek.

On my advance in Second—feint cheek, cut at flank.

On my beat in Third—deceive and feint point, cheek, cut at chest.

On my change of engagement from Third to Fourth—deceive and feint cheek, point.

On my feint at cheek from Second—beat and disengage with point.

On my feint at cheek from Second—beat and cut at head.

On my direct feint with point—graze in Third, feint flank, cut at cheek, etc., etc.

Parries to meet the above examples and ripostes.

Advance—I disengage—parry Fourth and riposte at cheek, etc.

Advance—I feint point, cut at cheek—parry Fourth and Third and riposte with the point (chest, head, etc.).

Advance—I feint cheek, cut at flank—parry Third and Second—riposte at cheek (point graze, feint cheek, cut at flank, etc.).

Beat in Third—I deceive and feint point, cheek and cut at chest—parry Fourth, Third and Fourth—riposte by feint head, cut at chest, etc.

Change the engagement from Third to. Fourth—I deceive and feint cheek, point—parry Third and Fourth (First)—riposte at cheek (Molinello at head), etc.

Feint at cheek from Second—I beat in Third and dis engage with point—parry Fourth (Second)—riposte at cheek, etc., etc.

Feint at cheek—I beat and cut at head—parry Fifth—riposte at flank (point chest, etc.).

Direct feint with point—I graze in Third, feint flank, cut at cheek—parry Second and Third—riposte by feint flank, cheek, flank, or time-thrust in Third, etc., etc.

SEVENTH SERIES : COUNTER-RIPOSTES.

The Counter-riposte may be simple or compound and may be delivered in answer to a simple or compound riposte.

Examples.

Cut at flank from Third—I parry Second and riposte at cheek—parry Third and counter-riposte at flank (head, chest, disengagement of point).

Cut at flank from Third—I parry Second and riposte ar cheek—parry Third and counter-riposte by feint flank cut at cheek (feint point, cut at cheek, etc.).

Cut at cheek from Second—I parry Third and riposte at flank—parry Second and counter-riposte at cheek (graze with point).

Cut at cheek from Second—I parry Third and riposte by feint flank, cut at cheek—parry Second and Third and counter-riposte by feint flank, cheek, flank (feint point, cheek, cut at chest; One-Two-Three with point).

Combine these examples with the retire by the backward spring.

Etc., etc.

The Delayed Riposte (*Risposta con pausa*).

The delayed riposte is a movement which exploits the adversary's natural reaction anticipating his instinctive parry of the simple reply.

Examples.

I cut at flank from Third—parry second—I react to Third—direct thrust.

I cut at chest from Third—parry fourth—I continue to Third—riposte at flank (chest, point, head).

I cut at cheek from Second—parry Third—I react to Second (Fifth, Fourth)—riposte at cheek (head. chest, point).

I cut at head from Third (Second)—parry Fifth—I react to Second (Fourth, Low Third), riposte at head.

EIGHTH SERIES : VARIETIES OF ATTACKS.

Counter - attacks — Redoublement — Reprise — Remise—Counter-time.

Examples.

Counter-attacks.

On my feint flank, cut at cheek—time-thrust in Third.

On my feint point, cut at cheek—time-thrust in Third.

On my feint cheek, cut at flank—time-thrust in Second.

Etc.

Redoublement (*Radoppio*).

Cut at cheek from Second—I parry Third in retiring—
On Guard to the fore with feint point, cut at cheek
(feint flank, cut at cheek, disengagement with point,
etc.).

Cut at cheek from Second—I parry Third—Resume
Guard and redouble with feint point, cut at cheek
(feint flank cut at cheek, disengagement with point,
etc., etc.).

Reprise (*Ripresa*).

Disengagement with point—I parry Fourth without
replying—cut at cheek.

Cut at cheek—I parry Third without replying—Disengage with point (cut at chest, cut at flank).

Cut at flank—I parry Second without replying—cut at
cheek (disengagement with point).
Etc.

Remise (*Rimessa*).

Cut at cheek—I parry Third and riposte by feint flank
cut at cheek (feint point, cut at cheek)—On my
absence of blade, remise with point (cut at cheek).

Cut at head—I parry Fifth and riposte by feint point,
cut at cheek (feint flank, cut at cheek)—Remise by
cut at head (point).

Cut at flank—I parry Second and riposte by feint cheek,
cut at flank (feint cheek, point)—remise by point
(cut at flank), etc.

Counter-Time (*Contro-Tempo*).

Feint at flank—On my time-thrust, parry Third, cut
at flank (disengagement with point, cut at chest, head).

Feint at flank—On my time-cut at arm, parry Third,
cut at flank, etc., etc.

Feint at head—on my time with point, parry Fourth
(Second) and cut at cheek, etc., etc.

Feint at cheek—on my time-thrust, parry Fourth
(Second), cut at cheek, etc., etc.

Attacks and Counter-attacks at the Sabre-Arm.

The practice of the sabre is an art. At the same time it is a militant weapon. An exaggerated attention to the advanced parts in preference to the main target robs it of much of its character and may finally cause a loss of interest and enthusiasm. However, circumstances arise in which a partiality for the sabre hand and arm may be attended with profit. Thus, if the direct attack be employed it should be delivered out of distance and preceded by a beat or *froissement*. Again, against an elusive opponent it may be politic to reduce one's offensive to miniature attacks such as the feint point cut at arm, feint cut at chest, cut at arm, etc., in preference to the feint point cut at cheek, etc.

Finally, the time-cut at arm should be employed reasonably and prudently and invariably followed by the appropriate cover in addition to the backward spring. In this connection, the time-cut affords an excellent medium for developing the speed of the sabre-arm. For example :—

On my continued attack at head—cut at arm, parry Fifth—riposte at flank (point, chest)—retire by backward spring.

On my feint flank, cut at cheek—cut at arm, parry Third—riposte at chest (point, head, flank) —retire by backward spring.

On my continued attack at cheek from Second—cut at arm—parry Third—riposte with point, etc.

On my feint cheek, cut at flank—cut at arm, parry Second—riposte at cheek, etc.

Or

On my attack at head—cut at arm—retire by backward spring in Fifth.

On my attack at cheek—cut at arm—retire by backward spring in Third.

On my attack at flank—cut at arm—retire by backward spring in Second.

On my attack at chest—cut at arm—retire by backward spring in Fourth.

The Instructor will at the outset offer reasonable exposure, gradually lessening it with the increase of speed.

CONCLUSION

PLATES

By courtesy of Fox Photos " Film-at-Home News."]

See pages 7 and 8, article III.

THE RETURN TO GUARD

See pages 8 and 9, article IV

THE BACKWARD SPRING
(SALTO IN DIETRO)

By courtesy of Fox Photos "Film-at-Home News."]
See pages 58 and 59, clause 84.

THE BACKWARD SPRING
(SALTO IN DIETRO)

See pages 58 and 59, clause 84

THE "BALESTRA" ATTACK
(ATTACCO DI BALESTRA)

By courtesy of Fox Photos " Film-at-Home News."]

See page 58, clause 83.

www.ingramcontent.com/pod-product-compliance
Lightning Source LLC
LaVergne TN
LVHW051751080426
835511LV00018B/3293